Your Story

a writing guide for Genealogists

Carla
Jean
Eardley

HERITAGE BOOKS
2007

HERITAGE BOOKS

AN IMPRINT OF HERITAGE BOOKS, INC.

Books, CDs, and more—Worldwide

For our listing of thousands of titles see our website
at
www.HeritageBooks.com

Published 2007 by
HERITAGE BOOKS, INC.
Publishing Division
100 Railroad Ave. #104
Westminster, Maryland 21157

International Standard Book Number: 978-0-7884-0110-7

Contents

Introduction

You've most likely picked up this book because you've gotten hooked on researching your family's unique history. You may have spent months, or even years, compiling names and dates and memorabilia. The picture may not be complete -- and may never be -- but you're at a point where you'd like to preserve your findings in a written form. You want to offer more than a laundry list of facts and statistics, but how?

Many genealogists who don't consider themselves writers attack the problem by wrapping the vital stats in dull restatement: "Edward Healy, 1745 - 1811, Moore County, North Carolina" becomes "Edward Healy was born in 1745, and died in Moore County, North Carolina, in 1811." Others follow the archaic models found in nineteenth century memoirs and family documents. Still more throw up their hands in despair and fall back on distributing copies of family group sheets.

You probably find none of these alternatives appealing. You want your family history to be lively, entertaining and informative --- to celebrate your family as well as to record its past. But you're intimidated by the prospect of turning information into story. After all, you aren't a storyteller -- or are you?

Today the art of storytelling may not carry the aura of magic it once did, but its wonder remains, so much so that most people are convinced that the ability to make a story is beyond their grasp. And so storytelling is left to the "experts" -- journalists and novelists who bring our facts to life for us.

It's true, the professionals know the secrets of turning raw data into compelling narrative. But in many ways, the spiritual heirs of yesterday's minstrels and storymen are the genealogists, whose task is not simply to revive and preserve a shared past -- not only to report, but to find meaning; not only to list, but to unify.

YOUR STORY: A WRITING GUIDE FOR GENEALOGISTS shows how to shape family data into a satisfying story that keeps readers turning pages. Even if you haven't written anything more ambitious than a long letter in years, you can learn to apply the essentials of the storyteller's art to the family data you've so diligently collected -- and produce a text that does justice to the people whose lives you plan to chronicle.

To introduce you to genealogical storytelling, I've gathered the writing fundamentals I've used throughout years of teaching adults to write, and adapted them to the special strategies I use as a freelance writer working on a variety of historical and genealogical projects.

YOUR STORY begins with the basic elements of a story -- CHARACTERS, CONFLICT, CONTEXT and COHESION. As you work through the stages of the writing process -- from prewriting to polishing and publishing -- you'll learn how to apply these concepts to shape material together into a satisfying and well-formed narrative that goes beyond a simple recitation of bare facts.

There are as many variants on the family history as there are families, and *YOUR STORY* demonstrates how to apply story techniques to a range of projects, from the traditional, comprehensive history to smaller, specialized tale collections and theme pieces. You'll learn how to find the many different stories in your family data, and how to create "spinoffs" of your base project for a variety of interests and purposes.

Part One: SEEING STORY SHAPES introduces you to the elements which are essential to a satisfying story -- whether it's fiction or nonfiction. You'll learn how to bind these elements together through themes and narrative threads that appeal to readers' subconscious awareness of the shape of a story . You'll prepare to look at your family data from a new viewpoint -- that of writer, rather than researcher.

In Part Two: GETTING READY TO WRITE, you'll work through the prewriting tasks that lay the foundation of your project -- seeing the "big picture" of the world you'll be writing about, and your ancestors' place in that world, as well as examining your material from the writer's perspective. You'll use brainstorming strategies adapted for genealogical writing to get your ideas on the page and make the drafting stages less intimidating.

Part Three: BUILDING A STORY BASE guides you through the process of structuring your text: shaping themes and facts into the actual story form. Here you'll create the framework into which your text will fit as you survey the many options -- drawn from successful fiction and non-fiction technique -- for arranging narrative elements.

To give your project substance, depth and reader satisfaction, you'll need to look beyond bare statistics and facts and create context and detail which give them meaning. In Part Four: FILLING IN THE PICTURE, you'll learn how to build in the background and foreground information that completes a well-shaped story. You'll learn how to touch readers emotionally as well as intellectually by appealing to their senses and imagination. You'll survey the surprising range of sources to draw upon for details small and large to flesh out the skeleton you've been working on.

At last, you're ready to begin drafting, and Part Five: TURNING NOTES INTO TEXT shows you how to handle that all-important first narrative version of your material. You'll discover how to find the writer's voice that suits your project, and how to avoid common pitfalls for genealogical writing, such as viewpoint switching, tense confusion and broken logic chains. Here, too, you'll also learn strategies for revising and polishing your finished project.

Part Six: LOOKING AHEAD takes you beyond your finished text to issues affecting publication and distribution of a writing project. Here, too, you'll explore additional ways to turn your family history material into a wide range of related projects, and to make genealogical writing an ongoing activity. We'll also look at ways to turn your skills into money-making opportunities through historical writing for a larger audience.

YOUR STORY focuses specifically on the concepts and strategies of story-based writing as applied to genealogy. So, for a general overview of the writing process and broader coverage of style, grammar, and publication information, Part Seven: RESOURCES offers a survey of related materials connected to writing issues beyond the scope of this book. Consult them for a look at the wider world of writing, publishing, and creating family history; in conjunction with the specifics of *YOUR STORY*, you'll have all the strategies you need to celebrate the story of your family -- the story only you can tell.

PART ONE:
Seeing Story Shapes

What's a Story?

Although the components of a good story might vary from culture to culture, it seems that at the core of every successful narrative lie certain elements that humans respond to. A very young child can easily catch out an adult trying to skimp on the bedtime story ritual. And older folk will slam shut a novel, complaining, "It didn't have much of a story." We may not be able to pinpoint what's missing from an unsatisfying story, but we certainly sense that some aspect of our basic concept of story form has been violated.

What are these essential aspects of a story? Setting aside considerations of "story" as a literary genre -- opposed to novels, plays, or poems -- the definition of STORY offered by Webster's Third New International Dictionary includes the following: "A connected narrative of important events ... an account of some incident or events ... a prose or verse narrative of incidents arranged according to their time relationships ... a narrative thread upon which a composition (i.e., ballet) is based ... an arrangement (as of pictures or tableaux) that in sequence ... tells a connected narrative."

Can you find the key? Note the concepts that turn up in nearly every one of these definitions of a story: "a connected narrative," "incidents arranged according to ... relationships," "a narrative thread," "an arrangement in sequence." More than mere information, a story reflects a deliberate arrangement of material for a desired effect. And an effective story needs a unifying, organizing principle -- the narrative thread, as Webster calls it, or, as we'll describe it here, the *theme*.

This unifying principle that binds all parts of the narrative together produces a well-shaped story, recognizable in its countless forms, from the much-loved bedtime book to the latest bestseller to a Pulitzer Prize-winning piece of investigative reporting. It's what elevates a text beyond a mere "laundry list" of information to a coherent work that's greater than the sum of its parts. And ultimately, arranging text around a controlling theme allows the writer to stretch beyond merely reporting events and describing individuals, and to interpret these events and people in light of the deeper connections that link them together.

A story is an organic whole. All elements are related, none are superfluous, and all work toward expressing the theme. That's a basic rule of composition which holds true regardless of what kind of writing project you have in mind. The story form is based on four elements, bound by theme, which produce the "big picture", the impression you want your readers to have of the text as a whole, and the message carried by the theme. Three of these are already available in your family data; the fourth you'll be developing as you work through the tasks in this book.

Keys to a Well-Shaped Story

If theme is the backbone of a satisfying story, then its limbs are the four essential story components:

- Characters
- Conflict
- Context
- Cohesion

All four are present in a complete story, and all complement each other to produce a text which has interest and meaning. Here we'll examine each in turn within the special framework of genealogical writing.

Characters. People like to read about people. For readers of all ages, putting a human face on an abstract point lends it immediate relevancy and interest. When fact becomes flesh, readers get involved. Journalists know it; the "human interest" angle gives depth to the neutral reportage of a tragedy. Scientists know it too, drawing on individual case studies to make their point. And certainly casual readers of all ages know it -- skipping over pages of lovingly crafted description to get to the "good stuff" of a short story or novel, or weeping when a much-loved character dies.

Good writing of all kinds relies on its characters. And characters -- a kaleidoscope of individuals stretching back as far as research will reveal -- are the heart and soul of genealogical study. Behind every name, every date on a will or a tombstone, stands a living, breathing and infinitely complex person.

Some of your characters are more real at this point than others. Your readers may all know Aunt Rose with her needlepoint and pearl earrings; the accomplishments of Great Grandfather, who ran for the Senate, may be well-documented in the local press. But even those who stand farther away in time can become vivid characters in your family history project, as you draw them into the narrative you create. And each one can make a unique contribution to the project, depending on how you choose to develop your text.

✎ _Conflict_. Tension drives a story. Many a play, novel, or short story -- as well as nonfiction piece -- has been criticized for lacking "dramatic tension," though all other story parts are present. Conflict -- the friction that arises between status quo and change -- motivates action and moves the narrative forward. It's the element that keeps readers asking, "What happened next?" and "How did it turn out in the end?"

Any change, small or large, arises from a conflict, or creates one, as people respond to new circumstances in their lives and cope with the larger events around them. A young man marches off to join his regiment in a far-off war; conflict, a break in the routine of his life, sends him away. Does he return home a hero, using his veteran's bonus to build a homestead and take a wife, and thus establish a new branch of the family? Or is he killed, and his family left destitute? Does he disappear from family rolls completely, with no trace of his fate? This point of conflict can have a number of possible outcomes -- but whatever they may be, the fact remains that as a result, life for the family will never be quite the same.

Conflict might be internal -- a man tired of the crowded town he grew up in makes the decision to move to the frontier; a young widow in precarious financial shape marries a man twenty years older than she; two brothers buy a horse ranch in Texas, or strike out for the gold fields of California determined to hit pay dirt. Or the tension may arise from outside circumstances: fleeing a war-torn homeland, a family endures weeks in the hold of an immigrant ship for the promise of a new life; a drought or famine forces a young couple to abandon their familiar surroundings for new hope half a continent away; government decision-making uproots whole tribes of Native Americans.

Marriages, births, deaths, land transactions and bequests -- all represent transition points that suggest a change, a break, a new direction for the family. These events can be arranged, like beads on a string, to provide the narrative line that lifts the text above a recitation of statistics. Finding conflict points and establishing the connections linking them is the first step toward laying the thematic foundations for your story.

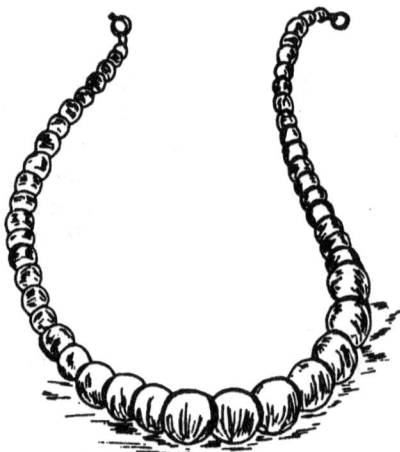

Beads on a string

✎ *Context*. People don't live in a vacuum. Individuals are rooted in time and space, shaped by their surroundings and, in ways large and small, shaping them as well. Placing family members within the context of their society and times anchors them in a larger reality, and provides a sense of depth and dimension.

The core of your family history project is the data you've so painstakingly gathered. But that material is most likely separated from its context like a stone broken from its setting. You may have noted that J. Daniels acquired 200 acres of land in the Carolinas in 1782, that he married Elizabeth Cowan in 1785, and that they had three children before he died in 1811. But as it stands, that information is completely unanchored in the context in which these events occurred -- the historical, cultural, geographical, and political reality of life in the late eighteenth century. To a reader unfamiliar with that period, the data stand in isolation, offering no sense of J. Daniels and his family as living, real people.

To provide context for family information is to provide that anchor. Contextual material sets the stage on which the lives of family members are played out. It creates the "big picture" that illuminates the individual lives of family members and reveals the significant implications of their actions.

Context works in two directions relative to the family data on which your project is based. One thread runs forward from the core of your project, the family, linking its members to the larger world in which they live. The other turns inward, to reveal the personal, intimate details that define individuals in terms of their daily lives. By developing context in both directions, the genealogist/writer can develop a well-rounded, vivid picture of family life through the generations, and interpret that picture in the light of the larger cultural and historical factors that shaped it.

Let readers know, not just that J. Daniels acquired his land and his bride, but that he did so against the backdrop of the aftermath of the American Revolution, when returning veterans were given land grants to encourage settlement. If your research has turned up a copy of that land grant, you might be able to note that J. Daniels signed with an X -- or that perhaps his name is misspelled, all personal idiosyncrasies that mark him as more than just a name on a roster. A little extra research might allow you to suggest that Daniels and his new wife kept a gun and a Bible -- and that frontier brides like Elizabeth kilted their petticoats to the knee when working in the field. That combination of larger context and up-close detail "hooks" the names to human beings and creates a picture of these individuals that lingers in the reader's mind.

✎ _Cohesion_. The fourth story essential is imposed from the outside by you the writer, as you make the decisions that build the foundations of your project. Cohesion for our purposes here means unity, and it's this fundamental relatedness of all the parts of the text, with nothing randomly tossed in and all parts accounted for, that provides the basic story shape.

A well-shaped story, whether it's fiction or non-fiction, has a beginning, a middle and an end. All parts of the story have some clear connection to its theme; they're included because they advance that theme in some way, big or small, and contribute to the overall effect the writer wants to produce. For example, a sensitive piece on the struggles of the first Feldmans in 1850s New York isn't served by a long digression on the restaurant Isaac Feldman opened in 1957, but a discussion of the restaurant business in the economy of 1853 might help show the odds against success.

Similarly, a coherent text ties up its loose ends. Of course, it's not possible to have all the answers to the questions raised by genealogical research -- some family members will always be unaccounted for, and some mysteries never solved. But you don't have to leave readers frustrated because their sense of closure has been violated by text that reads like this: "August Gladner had three sons: Charles (born 1844), Elijah (born 1846) and Nathan (born 1850). Charles remained in Dearborn all his life, joining his uncle Seth's law practice. Elijah joined the Army and was posted to the Arizona territory, where in 1874 he was killed in a skirmish with the Apache."

Readers who stick with you to the end of this paragraph may well be left with a nagging sense of incompleteness: August had three sons, didn't he? What happened to Nathan? You may not know; all efforts to account for Nathan may have come to naught. But you can ensure cohesion for the narrative about this particular branch of the Gladner family by acknowledging this fact: "Nothing further is known about Nathan Gladner." This way you've accounted for all parts of the story and demonstrated that you didn't simply forget to follow up on Nathan as you did with his brothers.

Another aspect of cohesion is consistency on all levels -- from mechanical things like style and grammar to larger issues of the narrative form:

    ✗ Did you begin with a flashback and then forget to flash forward?

    ✗ Are your readers constantly confused about when and where they are in the text?

    ✗ Do you veer wildly from topic to topic without any transitions or justification?

Any glitches or lapses that violate the basic unity of the material, and prevent readers from getting your intended message, threaten cohesion.

Theme: The Tie That Binds

At this point, your raw material --the data you've been compiling on family members -- may seem like pieces in a jigsaw puzzle: connected in a general way by the notion of "family," but otherwise a jumble of discrete pieces of information that can only be managed by lining them up in strict chronological sequence.

If you arrange the pieces of your jigsaw puzzle in a line, you still won't have the big picture. You'll account for all your pieces, but you've ignored the connections, the ways in which they fit together to provide a view of something bigger than themselves. So it is with genealogical material: simply putting family facts into chronological order without regard to the big picture that information implies won't give the reader the sense of structure offered by a story, and can't begin to reveal the depth and the connections hidden in the material.

Theme, as we suggested earlier, is the thread that works to bind Character, Conflict, Context to achieve the Cohesion that leads to a well-shaped and satisfying story. Finding and using the thematic connections in your material can open up a whole new world of options for developing your family history.

Journalists learn to develop a news piece around questions: the five _Ws_ -- WHO, WHAT, WHEN, WHERE, WHY -- and one _H_ -- HOW -- make sure that all aspects of a story are accounted for. For the genealogist/writer, WHO, WHAT, WHEN and WHERE are answered in some way by the family data, in combination perhaps with some additional research for context and details. The more elusive WHY and HOW can be addressed by the themes you find beneath the bits of information you've collected.

Where does the family historian look for theme? The key to finding thematic links in your family history is commonality -- identifying those elements that link family members in some larger way and, taken as a whole, reveal a clearer picture of them and their lives.

Your themes can be from outside -- corresponding to predetermined organizing principles -- marking off the text according to geographical or chronological division such as "The Crawfords in Texas" or "The First Settlers". This kind of simple theme may not reveal much of a deeper nature but it offers a serviceable structure principle that lets you break up the text into manageable units and group material efficiently.

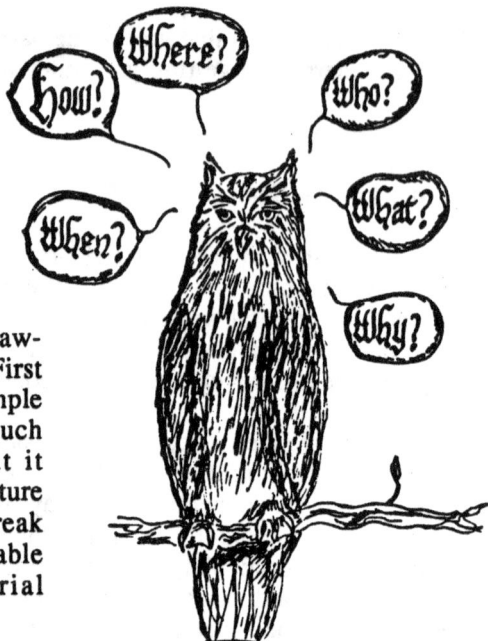

But the most meaningful themes emerge from the material itself, revealed by events and personalities you've encountered in the course of your research. Those impressions that linger long after you've put your notebooks away might carry the seeds of theme: are you left with admiration for those hardy ancestors who toughed out the early days of the frontier? Are you haunted by the mention of a ten-year-old slave girl sold for ten pounds sterling? Does it amaze you that your great-grandparents were able to slip away from certain death in the pogroms of their homeland? Perhaps you're shaking your head over the way your great-aunt raised six children in a dirt-floored sod house. Any of these strong images might turn into a theme: "taming the frontier," "women in slavery," "flight into freedom," "the Harding women on the frontier."

Repeating events can suggest themes. What if five generations of men devoted themselves to the clergy? If every branch of the family was active in civic affairs? If almost every ancestor had a large (or small) family?

Themes can also come from social or cultural phenomena. What effect did the Civil War have on all the family branches in the South?

Did the family have any particular traditions or celebrations? How did the Depression affect family fortunes?

Working from theme lays a deeper foundation for your story. It allows you not only to present the information you've collected, but to explore its significance and to reveal links that your readers may not be aware of -- to form the overall structure that binds all the pieces of your family jigsaw puzzle.

You already have the characters who will play the major roles in your family's story. Your research has shown you at least some of the conflicts and influences that shaped their lives. Now take the data you've collected and a few sheets of paper; you're ready to begin the prewriting phase of your project, where you establish the themes and structure that will guide the process from start to finish.

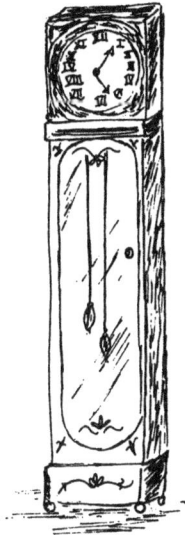

HIGHLIGHTS TO PART ONE

● More than information, an effective story needs a unifying, organizing principle -- the narrative thread -- the *theme.*

● Themes may be suggested to you by meaningful events (such as the Civil War), your impressions of your ancestors' personalities, a commonality that links your family members in some larger way, or repeating elements.

● Your theme enables you to create a big picture from all of your small jigsaw puzzle pieces.

● The keys to a well-shaped story are the four *C*s:

✎ Characters
✎ Conflict
✎ Context
✎ Cohesion

● The five *W*s and one *H* of good reporting are:

✎ WHO
✎ WHAT
✎ WHEN
✎ WHERE
✎ WHY
✎ HOW

PART TWO:
Getting Ready To Write

---

*Y*ou've done some research. You're full of ideas about what your project will be -- so you sit down and start writing, right? Not necessarily. What appears to be the logical first step really isn't. As countless newcomers to the world of writing discover every day (usually after filling a wastebasket with false starts), plunging headlong into the text without a clear idea about the overall plan and shape you want it to take is an invitation to frustration.

Getting essential decisions out of the way before you plunge into the actual work of writing frees you from having to work on the primary level of structure and the secondary level of text at the same time. That's a task that can eventually overwhelm the genealogist/ writer who's struggling simultaneously not only with what to say and in what order, but also with how to express these key ideas and themes.

The writing job becomes much more manageable if it's broken down into stages:

- prewriting, which generates ideas and imposes structure;
- developing, which creates details and specifics to flesh out that skeleton form;
- drafting -- combining words on the page, and changing them as often as necessary, until the text has just the right shape, tone and content to suit the purpose you've set out for it.

Let's begin at the real beginning then, with a look at how prewriting can save your sanity and your project.

Starting Out

Every writer has favorite materials and methods for making writing easier, and your project will go more smoothly if you aren't fighting your natural preferences. If you don't write enough on a regular basis to have developed a set of comfortable habits, take some time before you leap into your project to explore the tools and styles that help you to feel comfortable, efficient and in control of the work at hand.

When and where do you do your best thinking? Are you at your peak early in the day, or do you come alive after the sun goes down? Does a steaming cup of coffee make paperwork go faster? If you can build your writing efforts into your existing "comfort zones" you'll find that the project goes much more smoothly than if you force yourself into a completely new routine because you've read or heard that it's the best way to write.

Think about the writing tools that satisfy you. Do you relish the speed and flexibility offered by computers and word processors? Or is it much more comforting to take up a good pen and some paper? Are notebooks convenient and inexpensive organizers or just unwieldy behemoths that can never compare with the versatility of index cards? Taking stock of the things you use now to accomplish your everyday paperwork and correspondence, as well as the methods you relied on when doing your initial research, can point you toward ways to make the writing job easier.

Once you've announced your intention to write your family story, you may find that others are full of advice on how to proceed. While you certainly don't want to categorically exclude new possibilities, stay true to your own inclinations about what works -- and don't make yourself adopt an approach that you sense won't work for you.

If everyone you meet says you must, simply must, invest in a computer set-up to handle such a big undertaking, while you really prefer the cozy feel of a pad of legal paper on your knee as you sit on the front porch, put off the decision until you feel the need for more sophisticated technology. Likewise, if a cassette recorder helps you keep track of ideas while you're pruning your roses, buy yourself a good one and close your ears to comments.

Individual preferences aside, almost everyone benefits from a basic collection of organizational aids. For large projects, a looseleaf notebook with dividers allows you to assign material to chapters or headings. If you're planning a small, specialized project, a spiral notebook or even some high-school type index cards will do. A pad of Post-it™ notes helps you tag material and assign it to the relevant position in the text. And finally, even if you are putting everything on disk, you'll need an assortment of colored pens and/or pencils, just to keep track of the notes you'll be making on your hard copy as you work through the material.

Know Your Material

After all the time you've spent researching and collecting the family data that will make up your project, you probably feel intimately acquainted with every last name, date and anecdote. But precisely because of that very familiarity, you'll need to step back and look at your material from a different perspective, in order to make the most effective use of what you have at hand.

Until now, you've been looking at this storehouse of family information from the inside -- through the eyes of a researcher, working on one item at a time and filling in gaps. But as a writer, you have a different task -- to step outside the material, as it were, and to look at it as a complete whole, a body of interrelated pieces of information that, taken together, present a complete picture of a family and the features that make it unique. Remember our example of the jigsaw puzzle? In the researching stage, you were collecting up the pieces. But now, you're looking beyond them to the photo on the puzzle box -- getting a sense of what impressions emerge from the existing information, at whatever stage of "completeness" you consider it ripe for writing.

Skim through what you've collected, with your new writer's eye. What do you have available to work with? Do you see a panorama of family history running from the earliest known ancestors down to the present, represented by individuals from every generation in varying degrees of detail? Or is your material heavily weighted toward a particular period or branch of the family? You may have a wealth of information on individuals living through the Civil War and beyond, but only scattered names from other eras and places. Perhaps you've had better luck collecting stories and traditions passed through generations than in getting a comprehensive picture of the family's entire history. Or you may have just begun, with a limited store of information on a specific period or individual that you want to document.

Whatever form your raw material may take -- stacks of documents representing years of research, a slim notebook containing scribbled notes about stories your grandmother used to tell, or something in between -- it's rich in story potential. Your first prewriting task, then, will be to match your data to a format that allows you to make the most of the stories it contains.

Finding A Format

For most people, the term "family history" brings to mind a stately chronological survey of all known family members from the earliest right down to the present; but that traditional, linear format represents only one end of the spectrum of models for genealogical writing. So even if your material isn't appropriate for that kind of project you can still write a satisfying family story in an alternate mode. There's a format to suit any kind of material you may have.

Stories can be organized linearly -- beginning at the beginning and proceeding chronologically directly to the ending, without many digressions or flashbacks. Or they can be structured non-linearly, beginning at the ending and working backward, jumping from one time point to another, or clustering events from different times and places around a dominating theme. Examples of both abound in fiction and non-fiction; a quick browse through your library or bookstore will offer you a wide range of samples to consider.

Family history, by its very nature, lends itself to linear formats. Most writers who have collected enough information to envision a comprehensive portrait of the family choose to work from point A directly to point Z, moving from generation to generation through the earliest days right down to the present. This technique also works well for smaller pieces of text -- "The Civil War Years," "The First Crowleys in Kentucky," and so forth. Of course, these small texts can also be strung together under a larger controlling theme, but still chronological order provides the organizing principle relative to the theme.

If linear models rely on the organizing principle of chronology, the non-linear formats for developing the family history proceed from a sense of hierarchy -- focusing on a striking or significant element and arranging the other parts of the text in relation to that key point. It's this kind of structure that lies at the heart of much feature writing, "color" reportage and fiction.

This approach lets you highlight theme, and to point up elements that you -- in your role as interpreter, not just chronicler, of your family's history -- consider especially meaningful or dramatic. If you're working from a relatively small storehouse of material, or if it's heavily weighted toward a particular theme, you may find the flexibility of the non-linear model appealing: you can begin with Great-Uncle Henry taking office in the State House, and work backward to show how his childhood experiences brought him there. Or you can lead from the theme -- "Women in the Robbins family have always been self-reliant" and work back through as many generations as you can to show why it might be so.

Many projects work from the middle -- some combination of linear and non-linear structures. Once you've gotten your "flashback" out of the way, you might resort to a chronological narration of the rest of the story. Or you can tell your grandfather's life story while cutting back and forth from the favorite tales he told you when you were small. The possibilities are limited only by the material you have at hand and the vision you have of the finished project.

Setting Agendas

Every project draws its final form from the interaction of three key elements: the available material, the writer, and the reader. We've just seen how the nature of your family data helps to define the form your history project can take. But your expectations and those of your readers still need to be factored in to give a complete picture of what your project will be.

What are your plans for the text? Do they jibe with what you have to work with? If you've planned a generation-spanning portrait of all the branches of the family tree, but you find that your research has concentrated on homesteaders in the Carolinas around the time of the American Revolution, you're going to have to make adjustments. Similarly, if you were hoping to tell the current generation about the first arrivals and their harrowing flight to freedom in 1880s America, but you really have much more information on how the family weathered the First World War, you'll have to do more research or recast the theme.

Beyond simply telling the family's story in whatever form best fits the data, though, the genealogical writer may be operating from a hidden agenda that affects the outcome of the text. Acknowledging all aspects of your plans before you begin to write can keep you from ending up at cross purposes with your material when you're halfway through and something just doesn't seem right.

Think about what your family history might accomplish. Are you writing to --

    ✐ Preserve all known facts for future reference? If you envision your project as the definitive resource on the entire family line, you'll have to hold yourself to standards of scholarship and detail that a more casual handling of the material wouldn't require. And you'll have to develop a format that does justice to this undertaking.

    ✐ Set the record straight, with the truth about a misunderstood person or event? If your research has revealed the facts about a skeleton in the family closet, the theme of your text will arise from your efforts to lay an old family myth to rest. You'll have to muster evidence and detail to support your contention that commonly held beliefs are wrong.

📝 Revise history? Rather than rehabilitate an individual or event through specific information, you may want to cover up a bad spot on the family honor, sanitize a scandal, or cast a brighter light on someone's less-than-honorable deeds. You'll need to devote some part of your efforts to turning existing information inside out and reinterpreting available facts to fit the impression you want to leave with readers.

📝 Make a sociological or cultural point? You may want to work through family data to make a larger point about a cultural or societal phenomenon that affected the lives of family members, or changed the course of their history: the status of slaves in eighteenth-century Virginia, for example, or the hardships faced by women on the American frontier. For a text like this, you'll have to delve heavily into historical context and pay particular attention to developing the theme.

📝 Amuse or entertain? Some projects focus on the "up" side of family history, offering anecdotes and information aimed at showcasing the family's best qualities and brightest stars. You can inspire readers with portraits of admirable family members, or make them laugh with a collection of humorous events or stories. This kind of project requires a light touch and a very informal style.

📝 Preserve vanishing traditions and cultural values? Your project may be the last place readers can learn about their heritage, as older family members die and later generations are absorbed into the mainstream of national culture. So your collection of Christmas traditions or Granny's winter-night stories can provide a snapshot of the family's past.

📝 Bask in the glow of your authorhood? Your main reason for writing might simply be the act of writing itself -- to establish you as an authority on the family and the custodian of its history. The information in the text itself may take a back seat to your voice as the writer, but your stamp on the project, plus the admiration of readers, can be its own reward.

Once you've considered your reasons for writing, take a moment to see whether your plans match the actual material you'll be working with. Do they run along the same lines? If you're faced with a gross mismatch -- say, you'd hoped to produce an inspiring story of heroism under fire in the American Revolution, but you've got only a handful of facts to show any family member served in the conflict -- you'll have some work to do now to bring your vision and your data into alignment. But don't stop there; there's still the third element in this writing triangle to be considered: your readers.

Think Like A Reader

Too often, a new writer's first efforts are completely writer-centered: the text jumps from point to point, leaving out connections and background, emerging in a kind of mental shorthand. Why? The writer is using herself as a point of reference: she knows everything about the topic, has all the background available to draw upon at need, so there's no need to spell it all out. But a reader, lacking access to all that information, is as lost as a traveler without a road map.

Your readers count on you to paint a complete picture and to guide them through it. They don't share your familiarity with the material, and they may not even share your expectations about the project's final form. That's why you'll have to work to make your writing reader-centered -- look outward from yourself to your readers and try to anticipate ways to accommodate their questions, interests and expectations.

What is your audience expecting to read? Are you writing a short sketch to be photocopied and passed out at the next reunion? Or is a far-flung network of family waiting for the book-length history you said you'd be finishing at the end of the year? Having an idea of what readers are waiting to see will help you plan the form of the project.

And what do these readers bring to the text? Do they already know much of the information you're about to present, or will your data reveal many new facts they can't have learned from other sources? How familiar are they with the larger context against which you'll place the family material? While you can't read minds, you can gauge how much readers are likely to know about the information before they pick up your work, and what they'll need to know in order to appreciate it.

You'll have to decide for yourself to what extent you'll allow reader considerations to affect your project. After all, you're the one to determine its final form, and it's impossible to second-guess readers on every issue. Still, the reader-centered writer anticipates their perspective and makes sure that the text is coherent and free of confusing jumps and backtracks -- just like a courteous tour guide through the country of the text.

Transforming Plans into Words

Now add the reader's expectations to your agenda and the contents of your family data. Do they fall together in a general way? Take time to fine-tune. You may be dismayed to learn that to produce the text you want from the material you have for the readers who are waiting, you'll have to give up some parts of your data, or add more. You may have to reshape your vision of the project, or take off in a completely new direction, in order to achieve the effect you want. Before you do any actual writing, be sure that you're comfortable with yourself, your material and your readers.

You still aren't ready to generate text - although at this point you'll certainly be able to produce material that may fit the text nicely. Before worrying about finding words, concentrate on finding the form of the story; know what you want to say before you begin to consider how to say it. The second stage of prewriting helps you to produce the ideas that lead to theme and structure. If the parameters of the project fall comfortably in place, you're ready to start putting ideas on paper.

Writing texts and teachers always stress that there are many ways to get raw ideas out of a writer's head and onto the page -- and that each writer has favorite strategies to draw on when beginning a new project. If you haven't been writing long enough to have a sense of what works for you, here's a run-down of basic prewriting methods that might get you started.

✍ Brainstorm. Take a piece of paper and put down the first thing that you can think of about your family data. It doesn't matter what it is; just write it. Then write another, then another...free associate, let one idea lead to another, or not, but write everything that comes into your mind about your text. Go on for as long as you like, until you begin to repeat ideas or run out of steam. Then set aside the notes you made. Don't try to change them as an afterthought. Refer again to these quick jottings at another time. Your brainstorming sheet will show you how your mind, free of its constraints, is able to draw out the most important and the most striking elements of the family history -- elements that can suggest a theme or, if you already have a theme in mind, provide a framework in which to develop it.

✍ Freewrite. Jot down anything you can think of about your project and your plans for it. It may be helpful to begin with a sentence like, "In this project I want to..." or "What I want to say is ..." and then write as long as you like. Forget about writing conventions or organization. You're thinking on paper, just as if you're writing a letter to yourself. Continue until you run out of ideas, and save your sheets. You may find that you've produced some paragraphs, phrases or sentences that will fit perfectly into the actual draft text.

✍ List. Begin with an item of information -- a date from your family material, a name, a time period. Write it down on your paper. Then list under it, everything you can think of from your material or your knowledge that might be connected with it. For example, if you write, "Donovans, 1864," you might list something like this: Charles Donovan, died 1863, Charleston, South Carolina; Rob and Benjamin, served Durham regulars; Civil War years,Texas and South..." and on until you've listed the most pertinent information at hand. Let each item serve as the springboard for others.

Whatever prewriting strategies you use, remember that at this point you're simply generating ideas. Don't try to impose structure, to order things, or to polish up the writing. These are raw notes to get your mind focused and give you a clearer picture of the overall shape of your material. Once you've finished, set your sheets aside for a brief time -- hours, days, perhaps a week. Then return to them and reread them. Do any other ideas come to mind now? Add them to your paper. Repeat this cycle until you sense that your main focus points are on the page in whatever order you've written them. You may have pages of scrawled stream-of-consciousness writing, or a meticulous list full of details. At this point that's all right. The important thing is to allow your mind to roam freely in the raw data, sorting and combining facts according to their own inherent logic. When you've generated enough raw ideas to fit the scope of your project, you're ready to develop a framework to contain them.

HIGHLIGHTS OF PART TWO

- Break down the writing job into three stages:

  ✎ Prewriting, discussed in this chapter
  ✎ Developing, discussed in Part Three and Part Four
  ✎ Drafting, discussed in Part Five

- Use the tools and methods you are most comfortable with; computer or pencil, day or night, etc.

- Your perspective has now changed from that of a researcher to that of a writer.

- Match your data to a format that allows you to make the most of the stories it contains.

- Ask yourself the following questions:
  ❑ What are the expectations of your readers?
  ❑ Do you have enough information to back up your theme?
  ❑ Do your plans match the material?

- Ask yourself: What are you writing to accomplish?

- Think like a reader!

- Readers' expectations + collected material + your project plans = common ground on which to build your framework.

- Be flexible enough to reshape your vision of the project in order to achieve the effect you want.

- Know *what* you want to say, *before* you begin to consider how to say it.

- Use these techniques to help you generate ideas that lead to theme and structure:

  ✎ Brainstorm
  ✎ Free-write
  ✎ List
  ✎ Repeat the cycle until you're satisfied

PART THREE:
Building A Story Base

---

*M*any newcomers to writing, so eager to begin, may settle in at the keyboard or with a notebook, only to find themselves staring at the blank screen or page in a panic, paralyzed at the thought of ordering all those words. They seem to flow like grains of sand, smothering all the ideas that sparked the project in the first place, and resisting all efforts to force them into line. That's because the text isn't yet ready to be born.

Before you start wasting time and paper searching for that perfect sentence to launch the text, step back and allow yourself time to complete the prewriting sequence. You aren't ready to worry about words yet. They're the surface manifestation of a long process of shaping and developing ideas -- and the more thoroughly you establish the foundation of your story's structure, the easier the text-generating stage will be. So, instead of jumping back and forth between the level of ideas and the level of language, allow time to work out the framework of the text and to assign the family data to the relevant spots within that frame -- to construct a framework of ideas on which you can hang the actual words you'll need to build your text.

Your first prewriting task was to take a fresh look at your family data, and to find common ground among the available material, your plans for writing, and the expectations of your readers. You did some preliminary, free-association brainstorming to learn what key ideas lay behind your information. Now you'll tackle the second stage of prewriting: arranging available information in relation to these key ideas and themes you've discovered.

You don't need to think in terms of the rigid, intimidating outline form you learned back in English class in order to build a clear picture of the overall shape of your project. Rather, what you'll be doing is more like stringing beads in a necklace, as you make decisions, big and small, that organize the pieces of family data into a coherent whole.

What's Your Story?

As you took stock of your material in Part Two, you may have been surprised to find that your family data consists of not just one major story theme, but many small ones which, interwoven, make up the tapestry of your family's history. Each family member, each place, each circumstance has a story of some kind -- some more accessible to you, some less; some central to the history you want to write, some only tangentially connected to the current story.

At this point, you're still creating a skeleton for your project, on which you'll hang the "meat" of contextual detail and language. So the first thing you'll have to do is to go back to your brainstorming notes from Part Two, and with your writing agenda -- shaped by what's available and your reader's expectations -- firmly in mind, define precisely what story, out of all the available stories, you want to tell at this time.

It's true that the goal of the traditional, comprehensive genealogy is to account for all the available data. But throwing it in, kitchen-sink style, just for the sake of ensuring that nothing's left out, makes for a busy, helter-skelter text that doesn't really leave readers with any lasting impressions. By choosing your story line, and building it carefully along thematic lines, you can reduce the chaos that comes from giving every piece of information equal weight, and forcing it into the text just for the sake of inclusion.

Writing a family history doesn't need to be a one-shot project, though for many people, the idea of "family history" does imply a definitive work that stands alone. Although for many genealogists, one go-round with writing a history is quite enough, the fact remains that almost any collection of family information can be used again and again in different ways, to illuminate different facets of that family's life, both collectively and individually. Different projects bring forth different stories -- and different facets of the story you've already found (see Part Six, LOOKING AHEAD, for more information on alternate paths for family history). That's why your first step in laying the story foundation is to decide on which of the stories hidden in the material is the one you want to tell now, in this project.

Will your project be one of those comprehensive portraits of the whole family line? Even if you are planning to start at the beginning of known family history and work linearly down to the present, you'll still need to find your guiding themes. Skim through the brainstorming and inventorying you did in Part Two. Do you see any general impressions that characterize your family? You may find your story in ideas like "first for the frontier" or "committed to freedom." Your notes may reinforce an overriding notion about family origins, activities or character: "Overtons -- serving their country," "McDowells are found in every state of the Union," and so on.

Likewise, if you've decided to make your project a smaller special-interest history, you'll need to find the guiding theme that will allow you to develop the story you want to tell. For a discussion of your family's first years in the United States, for example, you'll want to concentrate on thematic notions connected with this period -- triumph over hardship, settling the frontier, and so on. Or, less traditional approaches might include tracing a possession through successive generations of ownership, reviewing the lives of individuals buried in a single small cemetery, or examining the impact of a single historical event -- war, famine, disaster -- on the family. Review your brainstorming notes for clues to the recurring observations that point toward a dominant theme.

Managing the Material: Text Units

Deciding on the themes that will bind your story together is the first step toward an organizing principle that will unify the whole text. Once you have your controlling theme, you can begin thinking about ways to make your project manageable. Organizing the mass of material into smaller units by theme and topic is one simple way to keep from being overwhelmed by the amount and complexity of the material you have to work with.

Remember the analogy of beads arranged on a string? Just as each individual bead, placed on the string next to others in an aesthetically satisfying pattern, contributes to the overall design of the necklace, all the separate items you've collected, arranged in relation to each other and to the themes you've found, form the complete shape of your story. And just as the beauty of the necklace emerges from the design composed by the arrangement of beads, the big picture of your story arises from the way you choose to present the events and individuals that make up the "beads" -- the self-contained text units that contain key events and themes.

Text units can be any length, depending on how you choose to break them down for your own ease of handling. For a long history, consisting of many pages, eras, and people, a manageable text unit might simply be a chapter, each having its own theme. Each chapter might be further split into subheadings. On the other hand, a smaller project might consist of text units as short as paragraphs, and a very small, highly focused one might stand alone as a text unit.

It's up to you to divide your project as you deem most convenient. But for the sake of coherence, make sure that your text units, whatever they may be, represent a notional whole -- that they have a beginning, a middle, and an end that allows you to make a transition to the next section. For example, for a project on "The Flahertys in North America," a writer might make text units out of chapters: "From Donegal to the James River," "On the Trail of Daniel Boone," and so on. But each of those units needs to be self-contained: Thomas Flaherty arrives in America from Donegal and with his brothers begins to establish a new life in Virginia. Once they're there, the chapter attains its closure -- all it claimed to discuss. Chapter Two, arising from a logical change point, takes the Flahertys over the Cumberland Trail and into new lands in Kentucky. That's the closing point; to begin discussing Michael Flaherty's move to Texas would initiate another text unit.

Likewise, any transition point from one period, place, or family to another marks a handy break in the text, regardless of length. Scan your notes for these change points; they mark the beginning, and ending, of stages of life and experience. They have a way of living on in memory and record because of their perceived impact on both individuals and the family as a whole. Purchase and sale of property, marriages, deaths, business starts... milestones like these point to human drama and movement, and form natural, self-contained units that form a map for the internal structure of the project.

At this stage, your goal is simply to find out what items go with what theme, what kind of text units might emerge and in what order to arrange them. So, turn to your notebook and your brainstorming notes. Allow a clean sheet of paper (or a blank card, if you've chosen to work this way) for each major thematic division you've found. Write a sentence or phrase that covers the theme at the top of the paper: "Makepeaces in Philadelphia, Revolution years," "Karpovskys endure pogroms," "Hamilton women, strong-willed, strong-handed" and so on.

Now, turn to the raw data. Skim it again for all the items that are connected to the main themes. Note them down in some way under the appropriate sections. You don't have to elaborate at this point; just make sure that you can identify the information in order to develop it later into a fully formed bead on your thematic string. Cycle through the material as often as necessary to catch all the relevant items and assign them to their proper place.

Seeing the Big Picture

After you've assigned the pieces of family information to their places in your theme structure, step back (figuratively, at least) and survey what you have, much as a painter eyes the image emerging on the canvas.
- ❏ Do you have a controlling theme for the project?
- ❏ Are all the text units -- from chapter to subsection to individual events -- connected to the theme in some way?
- ❏ Have you been able to assign most, if not all, of your family data to some point of your emerging framework?

You may find at this point that you have material that's left over, particularly if you've settled on themes that are more narrowly focused than a general survey of the family history as a whole. These smaller projects, really a subset of the comprehensive history, will by their nature exclude large portions of the data: if your main theme explores how the Ahearn families endured the Civil War in South Carolina, you'll have made a conscious decision to reserve the other information about Ahearns in 1830 or 1899 for another project. Or if your goal is to remember your great-grandmother and the Cajun tales she used to tell, you'll set aside other material about the rest of the family for the moment.

But what if you haven't intentionally excluded some portions of the family data from the project at hand -- yet you still have material that just doesn't fit any of the sections you've established? Sometimes, certain items may seem completely unplaceable: random, isolated people and events that bear no apparent connection to anything else. What about the black sheep who broke all ties with the family in Ohio and took up mining in Alaska? Perhaps one ancestor spent the whole Civil War jailed for desertion while his Confederate relatives collected commendations for valorous service. Or perhaps you've turned up some skimpy, unenlightening facts about someone who ran a hardware store in Arkansas in 1855 -- no more, no less, no impact.

We've said that a well-shaped story should operate on the connections that link all its elements. But faced with anomalies like these, you may be caught between presenting an incomplete picture, and shoehorning the mismatched information into a lifeless recitation of unconnected facts. Still, it's possible to find common threads that bind seemingly disparate items together. Recast the theme in broader terms, creating a bigger umbrella for a wider range of facts. Rather than devoting a Civil War unit to a discussion of how many family members served the Confederate cause, you might slant the material toward a look at all the ways the War touched their lives -- from those who fought to those who stayed behind, to those who refused to serve.

You might also find that a large enough collection of anomalies can be clustered under their own theme. The Alaska renegade might find company among others who struck out in a new direction, forming a unit around a notion like "mavericks of the clan," "new directions," or "different paths."

The emerging shape of your text may be lopsided, with some units which are very large, and others which are relatively skimpy. To even things out, you might need to do some juggling and restating ideas until you arrive at the divisions you like. Very big units can be broken into smaller ones: "Putting Down Colonial Roots" might cover several branches of the family at once; more manageable units might focus on separate family groups or even divide things according to historical periods or places. Conversely, some themes are too narrow to allow for much development. If you find that you've assigned relatively few items to one or more of your sections, you may need to recast the main themes in broader terms and reassign that information to other, related sections.

Organizing for Impact: Foreground and Background

By now your sheets or cards should be filling up: you have the major themes you want to develop, and you've managed to locate and note the family data you want to include in each section. Now it's time to begin imposing order on the information, and arranging it for maximum story impact -- stringing the beads to fit the overall design plan of the necklace.

As you've probably seen in the course of researching your family's history, not all facts are created equal. There might be pages and pages on the prominent great-uncle who founded a town and served two terms in Congress, but a scant two lines on his younger brother, who was a small-town physician all his life. People might appear by name only in obscure land transactions, with no further mention in any other sources, while certain individuals might be well-documented through letters and even books. Similarly, one family might sail through a largely untroubled - and thus generally undocumented - life, leaving the lion's share of drama to others, touched by larger events or shattered by disaster. Trying for an even-handed treatment of all is bound to leave the text unfocused and lopsided. But working from a story viewpoint allows you to deal with these inequities and to compensate for missing or skimpy information.

Since your primary goal in a story-based text is to advance a theme, and to create a series of dominant impressions (or perhaps just one overriding image) in the minds of readers, you can choose to highlight those portions of family information that are rich in details or drama by bringing them into the foreground of the text, while shifting the lower-profile material into a supporting role.

Every story is organized around a concept, a theme, a message. Some events and characters are central to this storyline, while others, necessary though they may be to a complete structure, do little to move the action along. Your task is to decide which is which, and to find the strong pieces to highlight for reader interest.

The place to start when you're prioritizing the elements in your outline is at the beginning. Whether you've decided to follow the linear structure of the chronological format, or a non-linear one that develops from dramatic points and follows other organizing principles, your story-based text needs a strong start -- a startling, intriguing, or even shocking lead to snare readers' attention.

Skim the data you've assigned to each of your theme sections. What events are "high profile" -- suggesting tension and change, drama or action? Tag them, perhaps with a number or a colored pen. These events and people will form the *foreground* of your text.

Of the elements you've marked, can you find one that seems to reflect the theme, or focuses attention on the issues you're concerned with in this text unit? Is there something specific that snags attention? Highlight it. You've just found your "hook" -- the piece that draws readers into the text.

Once you've found the hook, you can arrange other events and individuals relative to it, according to either the linear or the non-linear model. A unit on the theme of family connections on the Western frontier might begin: "William Taverty never had a chance to try out his gold pan. The novice prospector was shot to death in Reno on July 6, 1869, just a month shy of his twenty-fifth birthday." From here, this writer could arrange the high points of the text in a number of ways. She could move chronologically through the steps that brought a branch or two of Tavertys out West, or she could jump in time and space, to show how many Tavertys died violently in the west of the nineteenth century, or even look forward, at what impact events of that time and place had on the course of subsequent family history.

What makes good foreground material? Those change points we discussed in a previous section -- people and events that:

- alter circumstances
- suggest movement
- propel the fortunes of the family in new directions

Thoroughly developed with context and detail, they stand as focal points for reader interest, and taken together, embody the overall theme you want to present.

And the small items, the uninvolving but relevant facts, the skimpy details? All those additional bits that exist as isolated names, single line notes or dates that fill out the family group sheets but don't have enough impact or drama to carry the text forward will work nicely as _background_ information. Inserted where appropriate around the foreground events that move the narrative along, they round out the information and support the main points you want to make. And, by pushing high-profile material to the foreground and slipping in less important points as a supplement, you can pack the text with a lot of information without the numbing monotony of reciting all these facts as equivalent in importance.

But your decisions about what exactly makes good foreground and what's best left in the background will depend on what kind of points you're trying to make; foreground for one story may well turn out to be background for another. The patriarch who established a family line in the North Carolina of the 1780's might well be the central figure in a unit on "Putting Down Roots in the New World." But information on his wife might consist only of a name in a will and a death date in a parish register. Beginning from this premise, we can focus the text on the man himself while slipping in the known information about his wife as background to the main narrative point:

"By the time the United States was ten years old, Benjamin Steward owned five hundred acres of prime land in the Carolina hills, much of it granted as compensation for his service during the War of Independence. When he died in 1799, his holdings passed to his wife, Elizabeth, who outlived her husband by five years, and to his children, Aaron, Benjamin and William. In the decades that followed their father's death, Benjamin Steward's sons increased the size of the homestead through a series of transactions that left the family with a sizable tract of land on the outskirts of present-day Durham."

_31_

Change the theme, however, and you change the focus. While the piece above focused on Ben Steward himself, about whom many facts are clearly known, it's possible to approach this same material from other angles that allow the writer to bring other information into the foreground and push Ben into the background:

"When her husband Benjamin died in 1799, Elizabeth Steward fell heir to the considerable properties he had accumulated since receiving his war service land grant. Under her trusteeship and that of their sons Aaron, Benjamin and William, the family homestead increased in size through numerous land transactions to a sizable tract on the outskirts of present-day Durham."

Skimpy information notwithstanding, here we've been able to place Benjamin Steward's family in the foreground while slipping the man himself in with hardly a mention. This second version might be part of a structure showing how Steward women can always take the helm at need. Other themes might shift the focus to the Steward children and their later life -- or to the entire policy of land grants themselves. Those are decisions left to the writer, and all are valid under appropriate circumstances. Whatever scheme you prefer, though, make sure your notes and outlines clearly reflect which items you designate as foreground and which ones should be background for this project. Number them to reflect the organizing scheme of your text -- linear structuring based on chronological order, or a looser non-linear format that arranges material according to relative significance. Or try color-coding the material: highlight foreground information in yellow, background in green -- or any other contrasting shades. Whatever method you choose to identify and "arrange" your text unit beads on the string of your themes, be sure that the status of each item to be included is clear. Don't trust your memory to sort it all out after the fact, when you've actually begun to write the text.

At this point, you should have a number of sheets or cards that contain a statement of your theme for each text unit --and you should be able to see, stripped of ancillary data, the emerging skeleton of your story. Now take stock of your project. How is it shaping up?

❑ Have you assigned the appropriate family data to the relevant themes?

❑ Have you marked each item as background or foreground information -- and can you order them in a coherent sequence?

❑ Does each unit end with a change point that can carry readers on to the next one?

Continue ordering and reordering as necessary, until you have a generally satisfactory story foundation that includes the information you think is relevant, in the order in which you believe it ought to appear. When you feel your skeleton text stands complete and balanced, you can turn to developing the context and detail that will put the meat on its bones.

HIGHLIGHTS OF PART THREE

- You're still building your story base. Don't worry about words yet.

- Plan the framework by using the key ideas and themes you discovered while brainstorming, etc. Arrange family data in relation to those key ideas. Think of stringing beads on a necklace.

- Break down your mass of material into smaller "text units". (Text units = beads on the necklace.)

- Choose your story line and build it carefully by reducing the chaos that comes from giving every piece of information equal weight.

- Make sure your story has a beginning, a middle, and an end.

- Scan your notes for *change points* -- people and events that:
  ❏ alter circumstances
  ❏ suggest movement
  ❏ propel the fortunes of the family in new directions.
  Use milestones such as deaths, moves, or marriages. They form self-contained units.

- Have a controlling *theme* (see Part One), and make sure text units are connected to the theme.

- If some of the text units are unusually large, and others too small, try to even things out. Juggle, restate; break large units into smaller ones. Recast into broader terms.

- Organize and impose order. Use a strong start to snare your readers' attention -- find your "hook".

- For maximum impact, separate the text units into *foreground* and *background* material. Insert background material around the foreground to fill in gaps and provide contrast between the important themes and the minor ones.

- *Change points* make good foreground material.

- You can change the theme and focus by manipulating foreground and background.

PART FOUR:
Filling In The Picture

Stories are universally appealing because they satisfy readers' appetites, not only for information, but also for experience. People are drawn to narratives that create an emotional connection as well as an intellectual one, and so a well-shaped story should wrap facts and events in a wealth of background and context to help readers feel connected to the events they're reading about.

Because of its uniquely personal orientation, genealogical writing has an automatic connection with its readers. They pick up the text not only to find out when great-grandfather came to Texas and built a ranch, but also to get a better picture of him as an individual -- more than a name and a few dates. And while it may simply satisfy curiosity to know the names of the first ancestors to arrive in North America, these facts take on a deeper significance when they're attached to real details about the world those new arrivals called their own. A reader who can envision a young man in knee breeches and buckled shoes, stepping off a wooden ship, comes away with a clearer picture of this ancestor than the words, "James Dunham arrived in Virginia in September of 1746" can offer alone.

A story-based family history, then, needs to be founded on one of the basic tenets of storytelling: bring readers inside the world you're presenting and show them that world through specific details and context that enrich their understanding of the essential information. That's your next step -- to move from outlining and organizing to the second level of story creation: putting the flesh of detail on those bare bones of story structure.

Think Like a Reader

Readers don't approach a text with minds blank and ready to be filled with pictures of your making; they bring a variety of past knowledge and experience to their reading. One of your many tasks as a reader-centered writer is to provide a place for that knowledge to go -- to develop the images that bring it into focus.

Mention 1776 and most people will instantly conjure up generic images of redcoated soldiers, tricorn hats and Betsy Ross stitching flags. Introduce pioneers settling the Kentucky frontier and readers raised on television are likely to think of Daniel Boone's coonskin cap and a tidy log cabin in a clearing swept as clean as Hollywood can make it.

But if a discussion of our ancestors' lives during the American Revolution or the taming of the Western frontier includes real, specific historical detail and background context, those stereotypes can give way to a multidimensional picture of a farmboy in a ragtag "uniform" of leather and homespun, marching off to meet the British in stitched moccasins, an ancient musket from the family arsenal slung over his shoulder. Using the same technique, the persona of the Kentucky homesteader can be developed into that of a family man who planted crops with one hand on his gun and kept his family with him as he worked, lest he fear for their safety while out of his sight. The reader's hazy, half-formed images take on new and unexpected depth once they're focused on the specifics you provide.

Similarly, putting events in context can allow readers to combine their general knowledge of family history with historical background that may paint a clearer picture of events than the family data itself can provide. For example, family members may know the story of how an ancestor traveled up the Red River to Oklahoma with his Cherokee wife in the 1830s. They may envision an adventurous pioneer and his devoted spouse, out to try their luck on the edge of a new frontier, unless you connect the man to his time and his circumstances -- a time when five Native American tribes and their Anglo connections were forcibly relocated to Oklahoma, moving north through a bitter winter's journey to a place they never wished to see. This additional information, working with the material already available to readers, provides a more complete and accurate picture than the family facts alone can offer.

Context works in two directions from your family data: outward, as background which establishes a historical and social framework larger than the individuals themselves, and inward, to develop the small, intimate details that characterize individual lives. Here we'll work with your structure outline to isolate areas where context and detail can augment the text, and to find ways to draw all these elements together for a well-rounded story.

Context: Painting the Big Picture

We've discussed the importance of seeing the overall shape of the text; of arranging events, both large and small, around a central organizing theme. That's the first step toward a vision of your finished project -- the picture on the front of the jigsaw puzzle box, if you will. The next step is filling in that picture with background information -- creating the larger context against which the family history is played out.

Contextual information draws from the vast reservoir of historical, cultural and natural factors which touch the lives of societies, communities, and individuals. Depicting individuals and families in the context in which they lived can illuminate actions, reveal tensions that lead to change, and place a unique stamp on their lives -- the lives of those who experienced the events of the Russian Revolution were shaped by influences very different from, say, the Jacobite Rebellion in 18th-century Scotland.

That said, where does contextual information come from? And how can it be blended into the family material that forms the heart of the project? First, return to your structure outline, and review the key events you've selected to carry the narrative forward. What do you already know about them? What do those dates or places bring to mind?

In the margins of your outline, jot down any impressions that occur to you. Or use a separate card or notepaper (just make sure you number these extra notes, so that when you're ready to write the text you can match the notes to the events you're describing). The notes you make may be a hodgepodge of memory, stereotypes from television and movies, or facts from high school history classes. That's all right. The goal is to have a starting point, a way to find paths for further exploration.

A key event in a section on the Civil War might read, "Edgar Harms died 1864 in Williamsburg camp. First Harms casualty of War. Widow moved to Ohio." Allowing your mind to roam freely over your stored impressions of this period might yield an image of Abraham Lincoln's solemn bearded face, or blue and gray uniforms splashed with blood. You might remember history-book details of how the war began or ended, or names of prominent figures from North and South. All of this material might prove relevant. But it needs to be sorted and focused in light of the themes you're working from.

Since you've been researching family data, you've probably also been delving into general history. You may even be a history buff, as many genealogists tend to be. But even if you aren't, all the information you need can be easily acquired in a few extra trips to the library. All you need to do is to orient yourself to the kind of contextual information that will serve you best.

In Part One, we considered the six questions journalists ask when planning and writing a story: WHO, WHAT, WHEN, WHY, WHERE and HOW. These questions can also point you toward the kinds of information that will contribute to a well-developed context for family data, as well as to creating the smaller characterizing details.

Let's consider our hypothetical piece about Edgar Harms:

- WHO were some key figures involved in the Civil War?
  Abraham Lincoln, and Robert E. Lee, certainly.
  But WHO else might have shaped events that affected Edgar Harms?
  WHO commanded the forces in Williamsburg?
  WHO might have had charge of Edgar's fate?
- And WHAT were other events in the world at the time, or in debate in the United States?
  WHAT happened to prisoners of war like Edgar?
- HOW did families of soldiers fare?
  HOW did they mourn the loss of their men?
- WHERE did the events of the story take place?
- WHAT was life like in that _time_ (WHEN) and place?

The questions could go on and on -- a new one arising from the answer to each previous one -- until you've developed the topic as far as the text requires. Then it's time to consider how to acquire the answers to the questions you've raised.

This kind of broad contextual information isn't necessarily available directly from the family data. That means that you'll need to go to outside sources to fill in the background of the story -- no difficult task, for context of all kinds can be easily developed with a little imaginative research. So take your structure outline in its notebook or card format with you to the library. As you locate information, jot it down at the relevant points on your framework -- or use a separate paper for an extended reference.

The most obvious place to start is with general historical information. Using historical context creates an instant frame of reference and allows your readers to plug in details automatically. To develop the larger framework of your ancestors' world, your first questions will center on WHAT: what was happening in the world in which your family members lived? What events were changing their lives, altering their surroundings? If your memory fails you, check an encyclopedia, almanac or basic history text to find out. Many provide *time lines* that cover not only major events, but also *cultural landmarks*. If you can't get information on a specific year that's significant for the family, try for the nearest big event: if a family member married, was born or died in Philadelphia in 1765, for example, you might base your context on the impact of events a decade later. Let readers know who was President or King, what wars were being fought, what major political changes were taking place at the key points of your story.

Historical milestones, while they may be the most obvious form of background, aren't the only kind of information that contributes to a complete contextual frame for family material. Use your imagination. Look beyond events to other elements that made up the world your family members knew.

What about geography? Begin a section on the first settlers in Arkansas with a description of the mountains they had to cross, or the river along which they built their homestead. Give a quick summary of the climate or terrain of the area, if it might illuminate some aspect of your theme -- a detail-laden description of a brutal Dakota winter, a searing Southwestern summer or the rugged mountains over which your ancestors hauled their covered wagon enhances your discussion of the determination and strength of your frontier forebears.

Natural phenomena can provide some unexpected and vivid context too. Environmental disasters and freak weather can change not just individuals, but the course of history -- the Dustbowl days of the 1930s or the Great San Francisco Earthquake of 1906 attest to the power of nature to shape human lives. Natural events of all kinds -- from hurricanes to eclipses -- can add drama and depth to the narrative. Major events may be included in almanacs or time lines. But you may need to dig a little deeper for specifics on local phenomena. More specialized, local history books and even encyclopedia entries on the region you want to write about are likely to have information on natural phenomena that affected life in the area.

Remember that background context develops the larger, external world of your story, painting a landscape against which people and events are placed. So with this in mind, delve into cultures, social phenomena, political issues; explore traditions, folklore and customs. Working from timelines, or general history texts, find out what people read, what music they enjoyed, what dances they danced and what foods they ate. Readers will have a much more complete picture of an ancestor's life and times if they know that while he was building his house in Maine, Mozart had just begun composing, or that _War and Peace_ was published the same year a young Russian ancestor was married.

In many times and places, a clash of religions or traditions led to persecution, exile or war -- or at the very least, caused tensions among families and communities. Show readers, for example, precisely why your Huguenot ancestors fled to the New World by setting these facts against the context of Huguenot beliefs and the cultural and political climate that prevailed in Europe at the time.

Placing individual acts in the context of larger belief systems or traditions also offers insights into the forces that shape people and affect the way they interact with others and their world. A description of how Jews in a nineteenth-century Polish ghetto celebrated Passover resonates with readers preparing to mark that same occasion in Pasadena today. And an Irish Catholic bride disowned by her family for a marriage outside the faith is better understood if her situation is explored against the backdrop of the long tradition of conflict between Protestants and Catholics in Ireland.

Be open to the possibilities suggested by the key events in your text. The situations you've chosen as the skeleton of your story might point you in an entirely unexpected direction for enriching context. You may find yourself investigating avenues ranging from how cabins were built to how gold mining was done, depending on the demands of the material. But don't focus too heavily on developing background context alone; save some time and energy for the other side of your task -- developing the personal detailing that will bring your story people to life as real and multidimensional individuals.

Detailing: The Fine Strokes

"Characterizing detail" is the kind of information that can be taken from the background context and made personal. It provides another way to describe family members as more than a handful of dates and names. So far you've examined the larger world of your ancestors, focusing on events and currents outside their immediate lives. Now with the "big picture" of your background taking shape, it's time to turn inward, to explore that other side of context -- the small, intimate details that graced the everyday lives of your ancestors and marked their daily connections to life and loved ones.

It's easy to see the connection between background context and personal detail in a piece discussing an ancestor's experiences during the California Gold Rush. External, "big picture" context reminds readers of when and where the call to gold came; it paints a picture of the northern California stream beds said to be full of nuggets, and describes the ramshackle camps that sprang up wherever someone was said to have struck it rich. Against that backdrop, the narrative can place the family of one James Bainbridge of St. Louis, who was 23 the year the gold frenzy was at its height. While the background places James into his environment, we still don't have a real sense of the man himself. But if we can get a mental picture of the battered tin pan he used to rinse stones, or maybe even the patched and dirty tarp he pulled around his shoulders when he went out to the river, suddenly we see him as a real person with a real person's depth and dimension. He becomes more to us than just a name and a few other facts, thanks to the additional small details that open up a glimpse into his world.

Collecting these characterizing details can be very much like a treasure hunt. Sources are everywhere, and virtually anything with a connection to the period you're writing about can yield some clues about the life and times of family members. We'll divide these sources into two types, primary and secondary, so that you can see clearly how to use both.

Primary Sources: Using What's at Hand

Primary sources for details are those that arise directly from your family material. You've no doubt come across a number of these in the course of your research: documents, artifacts, photos, paintings, or any other objects belonging to family members. If you don't have these handy as part of your data file, try to collect them now. You'll be examining these items again from a new viewpoint: up to now you've been concerned with what they say or who they represent, but at this point you'll be considering them from a purely physical standpoint.

An easy place to start might be with documents. It's a rare genealogist who doesn't have a collection of papers from past generations; wills, letters, deeds, even receipts and bills offer information on family members. They may be originals, carefully preserved, or copies from registers and official rosters -- no matter. You've extracted the relevant information from them; now let their appearance work for you too as a way to comment on those who wrote or signed them.

Start with what you see and feel. If you're lucky enough to have original letters or other documents, examine the paper. Is it different from the paper you're making notes on? How? What sort of texture does it have? What does it say about the circumstances of the writer or signer? What implements were used to mark on it? The parchment and faded ink of a seventeenth-century

deed speaks for its signer just as much as a Civil War letter in charcoal on scraps of brown wrapping paper.

Look too at the writing style and language. Handwriting conventions, spelling and grammar, all reveal aspects of the education, circumstances and character of the writer and his or her life. The pencil scribble of a young boy writing to a cousin in 1885 Chicago, the elegant Spenserian script on a handwritten deed, or the shaky scrawl of an elderly pensioner on a statement of military service can offer distinguishing detail about the writers. The lack of writing can also be significant: a farm widow's scrawled X on a bill of sale might testify to the lack of education for women in the rural America of 1855, or to the signer's age or infirmity.

Books, too, are wonderful sources of physical detail, not just information. An old family Bible with its cracked leather cover and torn, tissue-thin pages reveals as much about its years of loving use as it does about the dates and names inside. Describe the ornate Victorian style and embellished title page of a family sketch circulated in 1880, and it's linked firmly to its time -- a time readers can now envision more easily.

Many family historians are fortunate enough to have access to images of the past: photographs, sketches or paintings preserve a vanished lifestyle that you can bring to life again through observing the physical details captured in the image. If you have access to any of these things, examine them now, not just to see the faces of your past -- though a direct description of family members is certainly the easiest of all detail to provide! -- but to find the small details that personalize people.

Ask yourself some questions again:
- What do the people look like?
- How are they dressed?
- Where are they?
- What kind of occasion is depicted?
- What period of time is represented?

A close look at Grandmother's wedding picture inspires you to describe her hands full of roses and the dress with its high collar, sprigs and lace -- or Grandfather's solemn stare and slicked-down hair. A faded tintype in its lily-bordered frame reveals more than simply the identity of those captured on its sepia face; the doll a child is clutching, or the earrings on a young woman in formal clothes, all help to characterize the individuals and their time. A hasty sketch can reveal specifics of dress, hairstyle and clothing -- and those early newspaper photos of men in bowler hats and high collars give you the opportunity to note their stiff poses as well as their watchchains and waistcoats.

Even the physical reality of the materials themselves can be revealing. Whether you're working with a fragile photo from 1872 or a snapshot of your uncles from World War II, you can describe the quality of the print or the paper, the size and the vividness of the colors if they're available --just as you would with the documents you've collected.

Consider, too, other kinds of family artifacts you may have on hand. Any object can offer insights about its owners, particularly if it's been passed through generations. Jewelry, implements, clothing, personal accessories like gloves or handkerchiefs -- all have a story to tell. What can they contribute to developing a portrait of the people who handled or used them over the years?

Secondary Sources: Filling in the Gaps

What if no family sources are available for the detailing you want to include? Reference materials can help here too -- the secondary sources that are one step removed from the immediate family information. When you returned to the history books to develop the larger contextual background of your project, you were using secondary source material, since the facts you needed weren't directly available from your collected family data. You can do the same for personal detail; we'll talk a bit later about how to relate the information you find to your particular family circumstances.

To find sources for secondary detail, return to the strategies you used to develop the larger context. For every general history text or encyclopedia entry, there's usually a specialized text on some significant aspects of the topic: along with overviews of the settling of the Southwest, for example, you'll find on most library shelves a number of narrow-focus books on life in mining camps, women on the frontier, relations between Anglos and Indians, or cowboy culture, to name a few.

For fairly recent events, you may even want to investigate your library's newspaper holdings or archives -- publications from the past reveal more than news. You'll find out what people bought, what services they needed, what opinions they held, and how they looked.

Even if you don't have access to artifacts and the other kinds of physical realia from primary sources we discussed, you can look for similar items in museums, antiques shops and galleries, and then extrapolate to paint a picture of your family's life. A painting of eighteenth-century ladies can provide insights into clothing, hairstyles, or furnishings, even if none of your ancestors happened to pose for the artist. And a browse through the treasures of any historical museum can introduce you to the realia of everyday life in whatever period your ancestors might have lived.

Returning to our example of the Civil War-era Harms family, you may have no more primary source material than the dates and basic facts. But you can skim the card catalog at your local library to find list after list of books and materials dealing with that period of American history. What kind of detail would bring the Harms family to life for readers? You could focus on the clothing they wore -- remember those voluminous skirts Scarlett O'Hara wore in "Gone With the Wind?" or the long high-collared uniform coats of the Army officers? Try a book on Civil War civilian life to show you what Edgar Harms and his widow may have worn. Or perhaps a look at their domestic life would be relevant -- try a text on 1860s artifacts, or perhaps a Civil War exhibit at a local museum. A larger library -- such as a University research collection -- might even have Civil War-era publications that show how people looked, dressed, or acted. All these sources -- and perhaps other, specialized local ones -- can offer ideas for building detail onto the bare facts available about the Harms family.

Connected with the issue of using outside sources is the matter of acknowledgement -- making it clear that you are using someone else's words, ideas or images instead of your own. That applies in particular to published material (see the "Legalities" section in Part 6), but it also covers family sources and the data from official records. Be sure to note what you learn on your outline or cards. Include a tag on where the information came from. Long, comprehensive histories might follow the standard citation format of scholarly works and college papers, complete with footnoting, bibliography and format conventions as described in research paper guides. Or, acknowledgement of family sources and other unpublished material might entail nothing more than a reference to the source, dropped into the text at the pertinent spot: "According to parish records from 1725..." "Passenger lists for that year reveal..." "Mary Leewit's letter to her son describes..."

Whatever material you choose to use, and from whatever sources it may be taken, it's important to let readers know whether what they're reading are your words or someone else's. Direct quoting can perform this task admirably, saving you the effort of coming up with a paraphrase. Draw directly from your documents; let the writers speak for themselves. A quotation in archaic legal English can do more to establish a background atmosphere than any lengthy description of what happened. And the voice of that young soldier requesting extra clothes from home can make his case with far more impact than your secondhand summary ever could. Just make sure, by way of careful use of quotation marks around all the quoted material and explicit references in the text, that you've made every effort to give credit where it's due. Collecting your context material is only part of the job, though -- you'll still need to decide how to incorporate it into your emerging text.

Blending Details and Data

In order to create a seamless joining of the external, background information and the internal, family data, it's simplest to follow the "general to specific" pattern common to expository prose of all kinds. According to this model, the most sweeping, general, "stage-setting" material comes first, followed by the more specific, family data.

When applied to the information you collected while developing larger context, you can lay the groundwork with general historical material and then arrange the key events of your text against the backdrop it provides. Following this format, you might have openings like this: "When the Declaration of Independence was signed, William Carr was just eight years old..." "The winter of 1778 saw numerous skirmishes and a number of outright battles between the troops of the Crown and the American militia. Whole groups of young men marched off to join the cause. A month shy of his seventeenth birthday, Clellan Jackson marched off with them..."

The same strategy works with other kinds of background information too: "The years between 1834-36 have been called the 'Little Ice Age.' In much of the United States, bitter winters and late summer frosts jeopardized the livelihood of many farmers and homesteaders in the Ohio Valley. In the spring of 1835, Jacob Morris, facing another year of ruinous harvests, sold his home and set out for the fabled lands of opportunity farther west..." Once you've oriented readers to *place, time* and *circumstances*, you're free to delve into the family-specific information.

Return to context at logical "change points" in the text -- when you take up a new time period, for example, or switch your focus to another place. If you've just closed out a unit of text, move on to the next with a brief, orienting reference to background context: "...so, Harald Nelson moved his family to Chicago in 1868. In the aftermath of the Civil War, the cities to the north drew many southerners determined to rebuild their lives after the devastation of the conflict..." You don't need to write a dissertation on every point. All that's important is to add the information that rounds out the key point you want to make and gives readers a reference point for making sense of the story.

The same notion holds true for the characterizing detail you've gathered. You don't have to provide an exhaustive run-down of everything you've learned about women's fashions in 1807, or the foods a homesteading wife would have fed her family. Choose only the strongest, most vivid images and work them around the family-specific material: "On July 28, 1869, Mary Baird put on a white wedding dress with a lace collar and hem. With flowers in her hair and a bouquet of summer roses in her hand, she became the bride of Howard Swanson. They shared just two years of married life before he was killed in a factory accident."

If your detail material is derived from primary, family sources, your task is relatively easy: link the details directly to the person you're writing about. But what if you really don't have much primary material to go on? Resorting to less personal secondary sources can still provide the images you want to create. To help readers extrapolate from this more general material to the concrete reality of family situations, you'll need to make use of yet another strategy: applying the *concept of adjacency.*

In other contexts, this idea might even be termed "guilt by association." In other words, when two statements are presented linearly, one right after the other, readers tend to see a connection between them, even if that connection is never explicitly stated. *Humans need to impose order on clusters of facts*, and you can take advantage of this inclination to create a vital image in the minds of your readers -- even if you can't draw on specifics from the family data.

For example, even if all you know about an ancestor is that he received a plot of land in North Carolina in May 1796 and he had a wife named Jane, you can use your secondary research to give readers a glimpse of what his life must have been like. Of course, you can't know what the man had for breakfast, or if he petted his dog -- or even if he had one, unless its name appears in some family source! But if you've been reading up on the geography and history of the Carolinas, you'll know what May mornings in that part of the country are like, and what your ancestor probably saw when he looked out his window. And you may know that men of that time and place wore unbleached cotton shirts and knee breeches, so it's likely your man did the same. Even if you don't know precisely that Jane kilted up her skirts and strode out into the fields to help with the crops, your research tells you that pioneer wives nearly always did. So if you place your concrete family information in the middle of this kind of general information, your reader will make the logical inferences about this particular pioneer family.

Of course, if your genealogical research doesn't back you up, you can't really say, "Joseph Heinz owned a barbershop in South Bend in the 1870's. Every morning he'd put out licorice sticks in a little glass jar on the counter for his customers." But again, you can place the bare facts about Joseph -- barbershop, South Bend, 1870s -- adjacent to some material you've found in a book about nineteenth century American life: "Barbershops in the 1870s were meeting places as well as grooming parlors. People came to chat and exchange news, and barbers would put out newspapers and little jars of licorice sticks for customers to sample while they waited their turn. Joseph Heinz owned a barbershop in South Bend..." As readers follow the text to learn more about Joseph, they store that image of the old-time barbershop in their minds, letting it color the information that follows, even though you never said precisely -- because you didn't have that specific information -- how Joseph ran his shop.

The ways to insert detailing and context are as varied as the family history projects themselves. Let yourself play with different options as you work through your material. With practice you'll see where more context is needed, or where you've added too much and bogged the narrative down. In any case, make sure that the material you've chosen resonates with readers, and works with the family data to open a door into a world they've never seen.

Getting the Picture: Show, Don't Tell

"Life was hard for soldiers during the Civil War. Sander McNeil and his brothers and cousins who marched through Georgia in 1864 wrote several letters to their families describing the miserable conditions under which they served."

"Confederate soldiers on the march were often hungry and tattered. Troops had to resort to stealing food from homesteads along the way, and bound up their cracking boots with leather strips to keep out the cold. Sometimes an abandoned farm yielded up a treasure: paper, which they filled up with news, round-robin style, and sent off by courier. Sander McNeil, who turned twenty that winter of 1864, wrote letter after letter to his mother, asking for long johns and a new pair of boots."

Both of these paragraphs draw from the same blend of primary and secondary source material. But the second version is far more vivid. Why? The details are specific, sharp and evocative. They touch the senses directly; readers can imagine the cold leaking through young Sander's boots worn to holes from the march, sense the hunger that drove him and his comrades to scavenge for food, share the loneliness of long nights spent dreaming of warm clothes and family. In sharp contrast, the first variation bypasses these specifics in favor of bland generalities that deliver the ideas, but not the reality, of the material. Readers are left standing on the outside, absorbing facts, rather than stepping inside the scene to live the experience.

A basic writing rule, one that's particularly relevant to genealogical storytellers, is to SHOW readers what's happening in the text, not just TELL them about it. As we've seen, showing is allowing readers to feel the scene you're setting; telling is feeling it for them, passing along the high points, stripped of the sensory detail that helps them to draw their own conclusions.

Showing, not telling, makes the difference between writing that a room is cold, and describing the way your fingers felt numb and you longed for your heaviest winter coat the minute you walked through the door. *Showing* is describing a drafty log cabin on a bitter January night when snow was banked to the windowsill; telling is a laconic observation that frontier houses were hard to heat. Telling touches the mind; *showing* does that and more -- it touches the heart and the senses as well.

The more senses you can touch in your use of contextual material and detailing, the more vividly your story will unfold. Think back, for example, to an event you remember well. Chances are it still lives in your mind, just as you experienced it. If you think back to that time, your mind fills with sensory impressions -- how things looked, smelled, felt, sounded. All these combine to round out the picture lingering in your memory.

If your last, cherished recollection of your grandfather was the time he took you to the county fair, you might still feel his big warm hand in yours and the hot June sun burning through your shirt. You can still hear chatter and laughter and children shouting, and smell the straw when you looked at prize rabbits and quilts. Your mouth might water even now at the memory of that sticky sweet cotton candy. All these vivid images lie behind the bare facts: "I still remember the last time I saw my grandfather. I was eight and he took me to the fair."

So too, when you're setting down the essential information that forms the heart of the story, you'll want to bring out those sensory details that lie behind it. Expand the scene; don't contract it into a terse summary that robs it of its strength and impact. *Blend family data with imagination and detail to create a multidimensional picture of the events of your text.* And once you have the context in place within your project's outline form, you're ready to begin drafting the text itself.

HIGHLIGHTS OF PART FOUR

- Stories involve emotion, not just information.

- Bring events to life by showing, not just telling, what happened.

- The more senses you can touch, the more vivid the story will be.

- Use context to create a complete world for the story.

- Historical background paints a big picture that creates context.

- The following types of information can also fill in your background:
  - geographical
  - natural
  - religious
  - folklore
  - politics
  - traditions
  - customs

- Personal detail brings characters to life.

- Use your imagination to blend family material with historical detail to make a multidimensional picture of events.

- Both primary sources (the family data you have on hand) and secondary sources (outside information) can help you create a vivid picture that pulls readers into the story.

- Build detail from family heirlooms, artifacts and papers by asking questions about their owners, appearance and use.

- Take advantage of the "concept of adjacency" to build detail.

- Let readers experience the story.

PART FIVE:
Turning Notes Into Text

---

*N*ewcomers to the world of story-making sometimes tackle a writing job armed with a host of misconceptions about the whole process: good grammar makes good writing; you need a special "gift" in order to communicate on the page; the words flow like magic from the pen of the truly talented; it takes a lot of training to get it right. There's a bit of truth in all these beliefs, but at the same time, a lot of crippling falsehood. Writing is a skill that calls upon many resources, combined to meet the needs of the task at hand, under the direction of a clear guiding vision of the outcome. So, if you have a functioning command of your language and a clear idea of what you want to say, you can acquire a set of basic principles that will help you put the words you use every day to work in a readable text. Here we'll look at strategies to get you through the sometimes intimidating task of turning your story notes and outlines into real text.

Of course, control of the mechanics of language -- grammar, sentence form and punctuation -- is the most visible sign that the writer is in command of the text. A messy page riddled with obvious language errors loudly proclaims laziness and lack of professionalism. But all the perfect spelling and flawless grammar in the world won't save a text that's awkwardly constructed, jumpy, or otherwise jarring to readers.

Good writing begins with good thinking: a clear understanding of your writing self, your themes and the relationships that form the deepest foundation for the story. Thus prepared, you'll be able to move confidently through the drafting stages of getting your ideas into a workable format. Then, and only then, will you be ready to tackle the surface tasks of polishing up the syntax and cleaning up small errors. *Keeping these writing tasks separate, and dealing with them in the appropriate order, can save you countless delays and needless frustration as you begin to build your text.*

There are many grammar guides and "how to write" books in most bookstores. These will help you avoid grammar pitfalls and show you how to solve specific text problems. They aren't duplicated here. Instead, we'll assume you have access as needed to this kind of writing support (see RESOURCES for some recommendations), and we'll concentrate instead on how to apply these principles to managing the big issues that concern the genealogist/writer attempting to reach a circle of readers. So keep your outlines and notes handy, as we work our way through the three stages of text production:

✎ getting oriented to the text
✎ drafting
✎ and revising.

Meeting Your Writing Self

No two individuals see things in precisely the same way. And so, it's not surprising that every writer puts a unique spin on the material at hand. Unless you're writing to very specific guidelines that ensure an impersonal and uniform handling of the text, your writing is in many ways an extension of you. Your background, interests, views, experiences -- all find their way into your text, revealed by choices in structure, language, and tone.

The text you write is the product of the myriad of choices you've been making -- and will continue to make -- at every stage of the project. You're the boss; those choices are dictated by your outlook and values. It's this very fact that intimidates so many new writers. And so it's reasonable to begin with a look at you: the writer self, whose voice and personality shape the text and give it life.

What readers encounter in your text may well be the only "you" they'll ever know. In the world of genealogical writing, of course, family members are the primary audience for your work, and many of them do know you personally. Still, the story they'll read in your family history springs from you talking on paper, and the voice that's captured on paper may well be a far cry from the one they're used to hearing: a blending of your own personality and the demands of the story you want to tell. Before you begin drafting, take a few minutes to get acquainted with your writer self and the voices it can call upon to tell the family's story.

What kind of voices have you used for past writing tasks? Just as you'd use different speaking voices when you're locked into a heated argument, giving an important presentation, or comforting a crying child, so too your writing voice for a chatty letter to Aunt Anna differs from the one you'd adopt in a report for your boss, or in the diary you keep for your eyes alone.

Whether you're shouting, murmuring or lecturing, your speaking voice always retains its individual timbre, so that it's readily identifiable as yours. Likewise, your writing voice will always retain its unique personal stamp, marked by pet phrases, a taste for short punchy sentences or long convoluted ones, a love of vivid adjectives and descriptive passages or spare unadorned narrative -- or any combination of elements that you find comfortable and appropriate. But just as your real voice is modified by the demands of the moment -- volume, speed, pitch -- your basic writing voice will be affected by those old familiar factors: the story material and your writing agenda.

Consider these two approaches to an observation about Civil War-era life: "In the aftermath of the Civil War, Confederate households were forced to endure severe economic hardship and domestic disruption." "After the Civil War, many Confederate families had to suffer shortages of food and fuel." These two writers are working from the same data, but they clearly have different goals in mind. The first text is distant, impersonal; the vocabulary is elevated, full of polysyllables and abstract words. But the second gives a very different impression. This piece -- short, direct and conversational -- relies on short, specific words and direct imagery: "families" rather than "households" and "food and fuel" instead of "economic hardship."

If you've envisioned your project as a comprehensive, scholarly tome to stand with other historical references, and your anticipated readers are awaiting just such a text, you'll have organized your story structure with that goal in mind. And your writing voice will have to follow suit, stepping up to, if not the level of the frostiest academic language, at least something more formal than the average conversational mode. But you may find that the available versions of your writing voice don't include this kind of scholarly exposition; most of your writing tasks have called for the chatty, informal voice of personal letters and birthday cards, and you may well feel uneasy about adopting the scholarly mode of narrative.

At the other extreme, if your readers are looking forward to a light, entertaining collection of family anecdotes to skim while eating their reunion dessert, you'll need to relax, put away the dictionary, and write as you'd talk -- an equally difficult task for a writer used to tasks requiring that impersonal, academic approach. Neither case is impossible to handle -- remember that you're capable of shouting and whispering with the same vocal chords -- but you'll need to be aware of how the demands of the text will modify your writer's voice.

New writers often worry about finding a suitable style and tone, though they aren't really sure just what those things are. Since we aren't concerned here with literary analysis and the subtleties of fiction writing, we çan simplify matters for these apprehensive beginners by simply rolling the concept of style -- a distinctive, individual presentation -- into the broader concept of the writer's voice: all those idiosyncracies that mark a work as unique. And as for tone, we can think of it as that aspect of voice that a writer matches to the emotional content and impact of the material at hand, in order to achieve the desired effect on readers.

When you developed the themes you wanted to pin your story on, and organized them into a structure, you were consciously manipulating the available elements in order to make your readers see things in a specific light, and to receive a particular impression about family data. Tone -- that aspect of a writer's voice that can be manipulated for effect -- is simply another device at your disposal for creating the desired picture in a reader's mind. Solemn, wry, witty, ironic, tender ... the words you choose and the way you arrange them are the window through which readers see your world. You'll need to be sure that they match your intent and your material, so that your readers get the message you intend.

A chilling recounting of an ancestor's harrowing ocean voyage to the Virginia shore demands an appropriately somber, and maybe even dramatic telling, full of color and immediacy. Similarly, a spicy anecdote about Aunt Lacey and the underwear salesman merits a chatty, upbeat narrative full of wry asides and slang of the day. The story would certainly lose most of its appeal if the writer took on a dry, impersonal academic tone. Likewise, readers might come away confused about why you chose to be so flip about an ancestor who nearly died in the hold of an immigrant ship.

You can even manipulate tone for startling, and vivid, effect through some deliberate mismatching with the subject matter. A piece about how Harding Sikes died deep into a frontier winter but waited until spring thaw for his funeral might be handled with solemn respect -- or with the macabre humor reminiscent of a mountain man's tall tale. It's all up to you -- as long as your choices of tone don't violate or muddle the picture you want to paint of your family and its story.

With an understanding of your own unique resources and the ways you can manipulate them, you're finally ready to plunge into the process of getting real text onto real paper.

Launching the Draft

Relax -- it's only words. They can always be changed, and they will be, numerous times, as you work through draft after draft on your way to the finished text. The important thing is to get those first words on the page or computer screen. That way you'll get past the stage fright all that waiting, blank space can cause.

Too often, writers find themselves frozen, searching for just the perfect word or phrase to launch the text. Or they toss down variant after variant, erasing or throwing them all out -- and maybe even abandoning the project in complete frustration. That kind of focus on getting it right the first time sets up a wall of performance anxiety that can make it nearly impossible to get it down at all. Writers who get stuck this way, and stay stuck, are confusing two different stages of text production: *drafting and revising*.

Draft text is never perfect. It's full of false starts, messy grammar, repetition and disorder. It's your first attempt to trap ideas in words, and it is to the writer as clay is to the potter -- raw material to be worked, and reworked again and again, until the result is satisfactory. The goal of drafting is to generate text. So start writing. And don't stop to criticize yourself until you have a complete unit of text, of whatever length you've decided your text units should be.

Still, getting started is the hardest part. So let's consider some low-stress ways to get you off and running. At this point, it doesn't really matter too much what you write. This start-up text can always be deleted later if it doesn't fit. Begin anywhere. Start off by saying something like, "I want to tell people about ..." or "I'm writing this history because..." Anything you can use to break into the writing process is fair game even if it sounds silly or trite just now. The key is to get past the blank page fright and keep moving. As you continue, more usable writing will emerge.

The key is to get past the blank page fright and keep moving.

Genealogical projects frequently begin with a "wraparound" introduction that lays out the scope of the history, offers a synopsis of the writer's background, or explains what motivated her to undertake the project. You might start with a simple description of the moment you decided to do the history, along the lines of: "When Margaret Van Owen was fifteen years old, she found a box of old letters in an unfamiliar alphabet in her grandmother's trunk. Learning to read those letters from her great grandfather in New York to his young wife in Greece sparked her interest in learning more about the family's Dutch and Greek origins, and decades later, in preserving its history for all to read."

Describing your project and what you hope to accomplish is also an easy way to begin: "Although the Hart family and its allied lines have been well documented for nearly 200 years, no attempt has been made to gather all these sources into a single comprehensive history of the family -- until now."

Another start-up strategy is to leap straight into the heart of a dramatic moment: "On his sixteenth birthday, Daniel Barr killed three men." From there you can move forward from this point, or backward to explain how this attention-grabbing incident happened.

For a more playful way into the text, particularly if your project is informal or unconventional, try easing in with a traditional storyteller's beginning: "In the beginning..." "Once upon a time..." "Many years ago there lived..." Even if you cut these lines later, they can get ideas flowing, set a tone and ease you into the body of your text.

Whatever way you choose to get into the text, once you've begun to write, don't stop! Don't get bogged down in fixing grammar or shifting ideas until you have a complete text unit in front of you -- one that can stand as a self-contained conceptual whole: a paragraph, subsection, or chapter. You'll need to see the whole picture before you can revise effectively.

This doesn't mean, of course, that you have to ignore all those nagging things that you know aren't right. Nor does it mean that you have to generate the whole unit at one sitting for continuity's sake. That may not be possible if you're working with larger blocks of text. But you can snare all those stray ideas for later consideration by making copious notes to yourself on the draft. Then you can return to the text to finish it in the same spirit in which you started. As you work, keep a colored pen or pencil handy. When your quick drafting results in awkward sentences or wording that falls flat, tag the spot in color and remind yourself why it's a problem. Underline or circle it so you can find it next time around -- or capture bigger issues with quick notes about what's wrong: "dull," "needs more color," "add in ..." Or scribble a string of alternatives; you can pick the one that seems right later, when you're editing. That way you won't be distracted from the drafting process while preserving your thoughts for the revising stage to come.

Likewise, when you reach your stopping point for the day, leave yourself a note or two about where you'll take the text next time: "do Parsons ranch next," "Harrison to North Dakota..." and so on. Some writing teachers even encourage students to stop with an incomplete sentence. Finishing that sentence at the start of the next writing session pulls the writer painlessly back into the flow of the text. Likewise, just taking a moment to read what you've already written can get your mind working on the text, and carry you right into producing new text.

Fixing small errors or simply dumping text that doesn't suit can come at any stage of the writing process as you read through your work. The key is to keep the text flowing without getting stuck trying to correct what you've said while you're still trying to say it. Your text will evolve over the course of many drafts as you circle around what you really want to say. Drafting is truly thinking on paper, and you'll want to generate as much text as you can, so that you'll have more to work with in the revising stages that will come later.

Once you've produced a unit of text that feels complete -- whether it's a chapter, a paragraph or even an entire short project -- you've got a body of material to work with for revision. So keep your red pencil handy and step back to look at your work with a (moderately) critical eye.

Cleaning Up: Revising and Editing

You can't revise text that hasn't been written. So in order to push and pull, delete and add and move, that complete conceptual unit is important. For just as the potter needs that clay to shape a pot, you need your whole text to begin revising -- imposing shape on raw material and refining it to meet the outcome you envision.

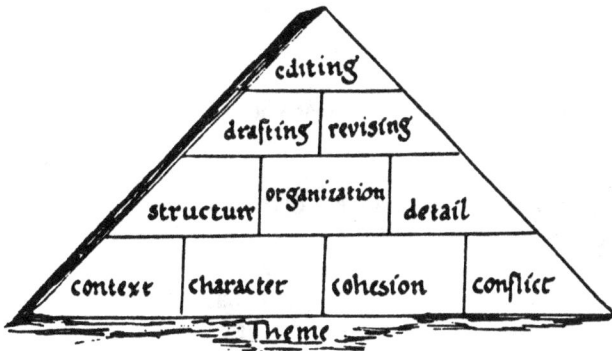

It's often thought that the writing process goes simply and smoothly like this: first draft to revision to published version. But most writers have a little more work than that to do, if they want the text to reach its full potential. So most writing projects develop through a repeating _cycle_ of reworking: first draft, revision, second draft, revision, third draft -- and on and on, through as many drafts as the writer feels necessary to get the right word on the page.

Revising is often confused with editing. Since the two jobs really aren't the same, you'll want to be sure that you do both.

> _Revising_ is changing the shape of the text -- manipulating
>   the ideas and structures that get across your points.
> _Editing_ is a surface job that takes care of errors -- spelling,
>   punctuation grammar and coherence.

In practice, though, you'll be doing both as you work through your completed text, identifying the changes you need to make.

Take the draft to a quiet place. Put your pen aside and read what you've written from beginning to end. You'll want to see the piece as a whole, in order to pinpoint major problems with arranging ideas, repeating information, or linking thoughts. Try to put yourself in the reader's place:

- ❏ Do you have a clear picture of what the text is trying to say?
- ❏ Is there any material that doesn't really contribute to that picture?
- ❏ Does one idea flow logically from another?

Go through it as many times as you feel are necessary to get a complete picture of the entire project.

Now that you've taken a look at your text from outside, grab your red pen (or any other color that stands out) and go back inside it. You'll be looking for specific problem areas and marking places where material needs to be added, deleted or moved, in order to make the text unified and easy to follow.

Any standard grammar/writing guide has a section on revising text, and from it you'll learn in a general way how to locate and fix just about any kind of story flaw. So, as we've done so far, we'll concentrate on just those areas that cause special trouble for the genealogist, thanks to the particular demands of family history writing.

Making Connections: Consistency and Coherence

Once you've gotten over your prewriting jitters and plunged into the text, you may well feel overwhelmed by the sheer number of words you have to manage, and the amount of choices you have to make at every turn. It's easy to feel as if you're wandering lost in a blizzard of nouns and verbs and adjectives, with the ideas that once seemed so clear in your structure notes nowhere in sight.

If you can't see the road clearly, then it's not surprising that your passenger, the reader, can't either. At least you have an advantage: you've seen the end of the road, though the image may be a little blurry. You understand the relationships among the events you've chosen to frame your story, and you can see how it will all turn out in the end. But readers don't have this kind of big picture view; they depend on the information you provide to help them make sense of the text. So if you hop from point to point without showing why, switch viewpoints arbitrarily, or jump back and forth in time, they'll lose track of the story.

Consistency in writing takes so many forms that it's not surprising that this issue alone can account for most of a story's flaws. Although every text has its own shape, depending on its length, scope and focus, the parameters of any well-formed piece of writing may be visualized as a ball of yarn -- solid, clearly defined, perfectly wrapped, with all the loose ends tucked in and no distortions in the shape. Every part feeds back to the central themes, and events follow each other according to whatever logical sequence the writer has planned.

Now picture a sloppily wrapped ball with bits of yarn dangling here and there, and the top bulging out over a middle wrapped too tightly: a poorly constructed text with unresolved threads of narrative hanging loose, story events packed in randomly and jumbled with unrelated material. This kind of writing leaves readers disoriented and disappointed; frustrated because they can't follow the writer's thoughts, they give up and put the text down. So _since successful genealogical writing depends so heavily on relationships between events, people and times, it's important to check yourself throughout the text for inconsistencies in both logic and mechanics._

The Logic Chain: Making Connections

Before you begin to work on the surface problems of connecting the elements of your text -- that's an editing issue that we'll discuss in a bit -- read it for simple logic:
- ❏ Are events arranged in such a way as to present a coherent image?
- ❏ Are the relationships among ideas clearly shown?
- ❏ And are all the parts of your story accounted for in some way, without any dangling threads?

You don't have to adhere to a strictly linear format to ensure that your text has its own internal consistency. Just make sure readers are clearly oriented to your framework. Consider: "In 1871, Asa Cook locked the door of his Philadelphia dry goods store and stepped onto a train heading west, ending the 200-year-old Eastern merchant tradition of the Cooks. Joseph Cook came to Pennsylvania with only a few coins in his pocket and opened his store." We're supposed to understand, of course, that these two events aren't simultaneous, and we can infer that Joseph was that first Cook who built a store in the Americas. But the fact that the writer makes us work for the connection might leave us feeling a little annoyed; the logical link between the two events isn't really established. Likewise, missing out on the relationship between context and key events cheats readers who need explicit guideposts: "Jane Tennell was born in the family house in Topeka on April 16, 1869. Tornadoes leveled entire communities in Kansas that spring." What's the connection between these two events? Did tornadoes destroy the Tennell house, carry baby Jane away in their winds, change her life in any way? Presumably so; but the writer doesn't really show how.

The Logic Chain

Making connections explicit is generally a matter of adding some transitional word or phrase at the relevant point: "Two centuries before..." "Now..." "So," "As a result..." "After..." To decide if the bridge of logic between sentences is sound, think not like your writer's self -- to whom all connections are clear -- but like a reader who's coming to your text for the first time.

A related problem concerns skipping essential stages, just because they're so familiar to you, the writer/researcher, that you never even think of them: "Lemuel Tolliver was the youngest of William Tolliver's six sons. When he was twenty-one he left Tennessee for the far

West. He took the pension money and invested it in a prospecting venture that failed in its first year." What pension money? Was it William's? Lemuel's own? The step that establishes the existence of the pension money (so that Lemuel can take it) is missing; the text jumps past that point and drags the reader along. The writer knows. That pension money was mentioned in Lemuel's Army papers. But on the way to the text, that information -- so familiar to the writer that she doesn't need to think about where it came from -- somehow disappeared, leaving the reader grasping for a connection that just hasn't materialized.

Consistency in your story also demands that all story parts be connected, both to each other and to the controlling theme. Unrelated material can derail the story and either confuse or bore readers, particularly if the text lurches off into a new direction.

Determined to develop the text thoroughly, and eager to write as vividly as possible, the genealogist/writer may be inclined to toss in any thoughts that are even remotely connected with the story -- and even some that aren't. One sentence leads to another, eventually taking readers so far afield that they may never return to the original main idea of the piece.

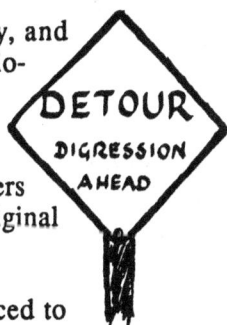

"The Santorini family's roots have been traced to Naples, Italy, the birthplace of Enrico Santorini, who emigrated to the United States in 1851. Naples is a lively city, full of the warmth of Italy and the smell of fresh-baked bread. The people welcome visitors with smiles and wine..." The writer may go on and on, bringing the attractions of Naples alive, until the story of Enrico and his journey to America has been left in the dust. Eventually, the text may circle back around to its point of departure from the theme --or it may not. At its most extreme, this kind of digression seems to take on a life of its own, carrying the text, and by extension its readers, far into new territory that bears only the faintest of connections to the story's theme.

Digressions and apparently unrelated information can still be managed effectively, if you've identified the point at which you went off track, and decided you'd like to keep those ideas. The remedy may be as simple as adding a sentence or two to justify the side trip. For example, Enrico Santorini's descendant could let that long travelogue about Naples introduce a new section describing her trip there to gather family data.

If the irrelevant material is still connected in any way at all with your main ideas, you may want to reorganize your premise to include it. If, for example, you've found that your section on the family's first home in 1870s Santa Fe has turned into a discussion about ranch life in the frontier southwest, you can return to your main theme and adjust it to allow you to show how the rough life you've described -- in lavish show-don't-tell detail, of course -- affected those new arrivals. Almost nothing is truly irrelevant; if it's worth keeping in terms of what it can bring to the text, you can almost always manipulate your themes to allow for it. But if you can't draw the unrelated material into the broader goals of your text without distorting its message and structure, take up that red pencil and streamline.

Another enemy of text consistency is the *dangling narrative thread.* If you've raised an issue, introduced an individual, or presented an event, *readers want to see them accounted for* by the end of the story, not just abandoned midway through. A story about how Uncle Charlie cheated the tax man isn't finished if all we read is that a collector came to his door one day. We want closure; did Charlie slam the door in his face? Did he go to jail? Or did the tax man buy him a drink and let him off the hook?

Of course, genealogy being what it is, many questions have to remain unanswered, or else your text would never be written! Still, you can account for the elements in your text simply by watching out for people who pop up and vanish, or events that don't come to an end. Suppose you write that your first ancestor in America emigrated from Ireland with three friends. You got that information from a letter, and you think it's a nice point, that the four young men set off determined to seek their fortune and share in it together. You add it to the text. But once the group arrived in New York, they split up and the three friends were never heard from again. How can you account for them? The best accounting when it's impossible to get more facts is a candid note: "Jack McBride never mentioned his friends again , and no one in the McBride family knows their fate. Their paths diverged once they made it to the United States." An observation that no more information is available provides just as much closure as a lengthy exposition; it tells the reader that you didn't just forget to mention what happened.

Losing Your Voice: Unity in Tone and Viewpoint

If you've decided that your project calls for a voice that's quite unlike the one that comes most naturally to your writing -- say you're planning a scholarly, completely researched reference history, even though you normally prefer writing chatty letters to friends -- you may find that you're wavering between the two without realizing it. A writer who's determined to maintain that formal academic mode may still "relapse" into a slangy, casual voice; alternatively, someone who's really more comfortable with the elevated diction of business reports and scientific journals might produce some awkward combinations when striving for a light casual touch. Be alert for strange collocations like "As a direct consequence of the vicissitudes of the war, the Barrett family bit the bullet and sold away the family home." Any text that includes in the same paragraph words like "gonna" and "intergenerational connections" might need some work.

Similarly, unless you've deliberately mismatched tone and content for a specific effect, make sure that your word and style choices relate to the subject matter: elevated and somber for serious events in the narrative, light and sweet -- or something in between -- for entertaining and upbeat material.

Switching viewpoint in midstream can also threaten continuity in the text. As you write, you consciously decide which characters take center stage, and which are relegated to a background role. Events center around these key figures; other things and people are presented relative to them. So, if you suddenly switch focus, you're setting the stage for reader confusion: "Chester Swain claimed two hundred acres on the Ohio River and built a house. He established a prosperous farmstead on which he raised corn and sorghum. Jonas Small had a hundred acres." The focus here has just jumped from Chester to Jonas without any signal. Are the two items -- and the two men -- related in any way? To keep a consistent viewpoint -- in this case, Chester's -- Jonas needs to be introduced relative to him: "Chester's brother-in-law, Jonas Small, took a hundred acres just downstream..."

Viewpoint shifting can also result from inattentive writing on the mechanical level too. It's so common in spoken English that we take it for granted. But in writing, jumps in pronoun form stand out like speed bumps on a busy street: "Howard Bitter left his family in Pennsylvania and set out along the Cumberland Trail in 1798. It was a rough journey to a frontier where life was harsh but land was cheap. You could homestead hundreds of acres without being rich." Who's "you"? Shifting from objective third person narrative in the first part to chummy "you" in the second breaks the thread of consistency that binds the text together. Even though in conversation we're used to using "you" to mean "people" or "one," on the printed page this kind of mix-up is an advertisement for writerly carelessness.

Other misuses of pronouns and referents can also interfere with text consistency and continuity. The writer, with all the facts at hand, and relationships clearly in mind, may see no confusion in writing: "On July 7, 1877, Peter Handy and George McHearn took their differences to court. He claimed his cattle were grazing on his land." Who's claiming whose cattle were grazing on whose land? The writer knows for sure, but a reader probably won't, given this string of masculine pronouns with a double referent.

Likewise, the ubiquitous and nameless "they" so beloved of conversational style and that catch-all "it" can contribute to a lack of coherence in the text: "They awarded a widow's pension to Miranda Hague." "Colum Neal traveled to California in search of gold but it proved to be costly and futile." Clear referents make both these sentences a little easier on the eye and mind: "The Army awarded a widow's pension..." "...but his stay there proved to be costly and futile."

Making Time: Consistency in Tenses

Readers trust writers to anchor them firmly in time and space. Since family historians work in at least two and sometimes three time frames -- past, present and in some cases future -- it's important to keep verb tenses consistent with the time referent and to signal changes with clear transition words and phrases.

You're looking at your text from a dual perspective: present time, the time of the writing and your commentary on all the events in your story, and past time, the time of the historical events in the narration. You can look at events from either viewpoint. From the present perspective, past events are seen in their entirety, beginning to end, rather like beads on a string. From the past, though, it's as if you're inside the time being described and looking at events from the perspective of one who lived then, and couldn't see how things were going to turn out in the end. Here's an example:

"The Krasny family continues a tradition of civic pride and community service that began in 1871, when Nikolai Krasny stepped off a cramped and smelly immigrant ship. He had been a doctor in his native Odessa, and he lost no time in setting up a clinic for his fellow Slavs. Since the days of Nikolai Krasny's one-room walk-up office, generation after generation of Krasny sons and daughters have followed his path, choosing careers in the health professions and community service."

How many verb tenses do you count? The text proceeds from two time frames: present, looking from the writer's perspective on the Krasny family as a whole, and past, looking at the events that actually happened in Nikolai's day. Not taking this kind of time shift into account can jumble the tenses and confuse readers as you drag them into the past with you and back again to the present, with even a few side trips into the future as you project past your own time into the next generations of the family. To cement the time structure of the text, you can signal such switches by using time adverbs and other structures: "Fifty years earlier..." "When Jeremiah Principal was thirty..." "That year..." "In May of 1909..."

A well structured piece is a tightly knit unit in which all the parts work together toward a harmonious whole that resonates with a reader. That means that one of the final, and most significant, tests of a story's consistency and unity is the *quality of its conclusion.* Your final words should echo the themes you established in the beginning and developed throughout the text, and leave readers feeling satisfied that they've gotten the complete picture. But all too often writers use the conclusion as a way to introduce a new idea -- one that really should have taken its place as part of the main theme too. Or, they simply stop dead when they run out of things to say, leaving readers waiting for a wrap-up that never comes.

Check your conclusion for consistency before you leave your text. Does it echo the main ideas you've established in the story? Does it carry the reader to a sense of closure -- and beyond, with a comment on the message that's just unfolded in the text? If you've just completed a text unit that needs to be integrated into a larger whole -- remember our jigsaw puzzle analogy? -- are transitions in place that lead readers into the next section? Try to leave readers with a sense of the key points you want to make: "Soldiers, statesmen, pioneers: the Newhalls of Tennessee have carried the family name from colonial Virginia throughout the entire United States. The later generations of the family continue the traditions of innovation, determination and courage that sustained those first Newhalls as they built a life on the edges of the American frontier." Here, we've distilled the text down to nothing more than its key themes. We haven't suddenly introduced a new thought about the Newhalls; that might be another text section. We've stuck simply -- and briefly -- to the essential points we want readers to remember about the Newhalls as a whole.

The Wrap-Up: Finishing Touches

You won't have a perfect text on the first draft. Or the second. Or maybe even the third or more. But continue revising, first, section by section, then, as you drop completed text units into their places in the project, the text in its integrated entirety. Look for areas that need more -- or less -- development, problems with consistency and unity, and ordering.

When you're fairly satisfied that the shape of the text is what you envisioned, it's time to move up to the surface level of editing for mechanics: grammar, punctuation, spelling and language use. Run through the text, grammar guide and dictionary in hand, until you think you've solved all the problems. And then what?

Do nothing. Put the text away for a day, a week...but not too long, or you'll lose your stride. And then take it out again. You'll see it differently now, with some distance; it will have separated from you, so that you may feel as if you're reading a text written by someone else. From this more objective stance, you'll catch errors and problems that you never saw on the first go-round.

Have a friend (or several) read what you've written. Ask for specific comments on weak spots. Then, when you've exhausted the writer's how-to shelf at your bookstore and read through the story until you've wrung everything out of it, when you know that you've done everything you can to produce a clear text -- congratulations! _YOUR STORY_ is ready to meet its readers.

The potter's finished product

HIGHLIGHTS OF PART FIVE

- Good writing begins with good thinking, not with perfect grammar.

- Keep the stages of the writing process separate. Don't try to plan, draft, revise, and edit all at once.

- Get acquainted with your own "writer's voice" -- how do you sound on paper?

- Ask yourself what kind of voice your project requires. Match your voice to the material.

- Draft text is your raw material, just as clay is to a potter. Don't get bogged down trying to make it perfect.

- Revising and editing are two different processes:

  ✎ Revise to change the shape of the text, its themes or main structure.
  ✎ Edit later to polish and eliminate errors.

- Let draft text "cool" a few days before you begin revising.

- Read it like a reader. Ask yourself:
  ❑ Does the text get across a clear picture of its message?
  ❑ Do ideas flow logically?
  ❑ Is all material related, and are all relationships made clear?
  ❑ Are all parts of the story accounted for?

- Have you oriented your readers in time and space?

- Keep a unified voice and a consistent viewpoint.

- You may need several drafts to get to what you want to say.

PART SIX:
Looking Ahead

You've typed in the last period, edited out the last typo. Your story is ready to meet its readers. What happens now?

For many family historians, that's the end of the matter. A trip to the local copyshop, or a manuscript sent off to the binder, and it's time to breathe a sigh of relief at having done the job, and to pick up all the activities put on hold during the project. But for every writer who happily puts the writing experience behind her, never to be repeated, there's probably another who stares in dismay at the blank page or computer screen and feels a certain emptiness inside, where the project lived for so long. If you don't want to abandon your newfound role as family scribe, you may want to consider other, related ways to keep your newly developed writing skills in working order.

When you began to plan your project, you were already envisioning the outcome, and as you designed the framework for your text, you made decisions aimed at getting to that end -- whether it was a comprehensive book or a short sketch. But in most cases the project you've ended up with is only one of the many possibilities offered by the family data you have on hand. Just as a popular film or television show might spawn a variety of spinoffs ranging from novelizations to mugs with the stars' likenesses, your family archives probably have many more stories to tell. Writing even the most comprehensive family history doesn't automatically preclude making other uses of the material you've so painstakingly gathered. And the possibilities are really limited only by your imagination and your willingness to write.

Creative Recycling

Any event, person, place or period you included -- or perhaps were forced to leave out -- might merit special expanded treatment as a separate project. The ancestor who built the family home in Virginia may have taken up two paragraphs in a standard history, but his achievements might be worth a two or three page "special edition" on the anniversary of his birth or death. And family members interested in the earliest known ancestors in the Americas might welcome a detailed piece on their culture and the historical circumstances that brought them here.

If space and time constraints prevented you from developing a theme as much as you would have liked, take it up in a "sequel" to the original, perhaps with some additional research. Or, look at your original material from a different thematic viewpoint: if you'd included a section on "Hardships of the Dakota Frontier," detailing the harsh life family members faced while establishing themselves in a new territory, you might want to return to the subject from a different angle: the lives of your women ancestors in that place and time, or their experiences with education or religion.

Those random bits of information you had to omit in the interest of preserving thematic structure might go it alone as a new project, suitably fleshed out, with a new theme. Or, background events in your original project can be brought forward, and enlarged upon, in a new take on the material.

Taking New Paths

You may also want to move away from historical research in its strictest sense, to take a look at other aspects of your family's essence: behind all the names and places lurk cultures, traditions and beliefs that shape family members for generations. Using your original project and its basic information as a starting point, you can explore the roots of cherished traditions, reveal the origins of family sayings and superstitions, and paint a picture of a cultural life from generations past. Family historians who've concentrated on producing a fact-filled text based on essential historical information might particularly enjoy a foray into the world of folklore, culture and language.

How did your grandparents marry? What did this kind of ceremony reveal about them and their culture? Did grandma bring a collection of ghost tales from the Old Country? Why does the family New Year's Day dinner always include cabbage? Questions like these can send you rummaging through your storehouse of family data as well as library materials for general background information.

Artifacts, as discussed in Part 5, can point you toward alternative ways to present your text. You might build a specialized piece around a possession that's passed from generation to generation, or develop a sketch around all the people who appear in a photograph or tintype. Let a Victorian brooch tell the story of its owner, or a pearl-handled knife recall the rough-and-ready Western frontier.

Stretching the Boundaries

Up till now, we've been basing our discussion of genealogical storytelling upon conventional formats that most historians are likely to work from: a book-style project covering a family's entire known history, a smaller-scale, informal sketch, or a mid-size special focus piece built around a selected theme or series of themes. These structures are the ones which come first to mind at the mention of "family history" and so they're usually the logical first choices of the new writer interested mainly in preserving information.

But with that type of project safely out of the way -- or even if it's not -- it can be fun to explore other formats and options for presenting similar material, and for expanding your role as family historian, if you'd like.

Some veterans of the book-length experience may find themselves ready to start another: "Family History Part Two," or a special focus book. If that's your interest, all you'll need to do is find your new theme, make plans for producing your final project, and apply what you've learned for a second time around.

For many, though, a second project is a chance to experiment, and to expand their developing skills as a writer and a historian. Here we'll look at a variety of possibilities ranging from simple reportage to creative projects that blend elements of narrative and art.

Family Bulletins and Newsletters

The most logical extension of the standard family history is the periodic update, notifying family members of new discoveries and adding to information already acquired. Many family historians rapidly acquire a reputation as a clearinghouse or repository of all the genealogical information collected by anyone in the family who's ever taken an interest in their ancestors. If you've become that person in your family, or if you'd like to take on such a role, you may want to consider producing a periodic newsletter or bulletin that keeps everyone current on research being done by individual members in different areas.

Your bulletin might tackle specific topics and themes, much as the separate sections of your history did, or focus on ancillary issues of interest to the family, such as a general history of the original homeland or an overview of a significant period in the family's history. Any aspect of the family data is fair game -- an expanded version of information touched upon in your original project, or new material that answers questions raised in it.

Many families use the newsletter/bulletin format simply to keep in touch. Current family information such as births, deaths, and other significant events, takes its place alongside genealogy pieces that solve the mystery of an ancestor's identity, explore the origins of the family name, or even share family recipes of a century ago.

Your publication can be as simple as a few mimeographed sheets tucked in an envelope, or as slick as a professionally produced newsletter, with the help of a computer and your local print shop. If you're willing to invest a little more time and money, you can include artwork and photos.

If you decide to make your genealogical writing an ongoing endeavor with this kind of project, you may want to designate yourself editor/publisher and encourage other family members -- and perhaps outsiders too -- to submit material. That way you don't have to do everything yourself.

Your newsletter/bulletin can appear as often or as seldom as you choose, as long as you're consistent in the interval you pick. You can charge a subscription fee or send it out free to family members -- the choices are yours, depending on your inclinations and the interests of your potential readers.

Once you've taken on the role of editor -- in addition to those of writer and genealogist -- and publisher of your newsletter, you may want to designate your enterprise a small press, either under your own name or a business name that describes what you're doing. For example, Anna Mikulic might produce her family history, newsletter, and any other materials under "Mikulic Publications" or even "Sunrise Press." If you plan to publish more than just one or two pieces, even if you're doing so from your own kitchen table, you can take advantage of all the services and benefits offered through trade organizations and publications for small press publishers (see Part Seven for resources). Be aware, though, that if you operate for profit, you've also become a business, subject to state and federal small business regulations. Check with your local business licensing and tax boards for specific information on your status.

Family Story Collections

If the storytelling aspect of writing the family history appeals to you, try creating family story collections based on tales and memories passed down through the generations. A compilation of old ghost stories, or family legends, might make a memorable holiday gift, especially for younger members of the family.

This kind of family storybook can be as simple or as ornate as you choose -- saddle-stapled from the copy shop, or produced in an elaborate hardback edition by a publishing concern. Other family members can contribute their unique skills too. Does anyone in the family draw or paint? Ask them to illustrate a cover. Is there a calligrapher in the clan? Maybe they'd like to hand-letter your compilation of sayings and traditions. Would a relative interested in photography provide some special shots for you? For the more creative applications of your family data, inventory the skills and interests of the clan. Some might be delighted to contribute in ways you hadn't even imagined -- ways which lighten your load as sole custodian and writer of the family history material.

Family history can be turned into art in other ways as well. Commemorate a specific event by creating a collage -- weave family history and contextual background among photos, artifacts or even old newspaper headlines to mark an anniversary, a family milestone or a historical landmark. The collage can be a family project on a big sheet of drawing paper or Bristol board, or a small piece suitable for framing.

Similarly, let an artifact or photograph take center stage on a piece of sturdy art paper. Tell the story of the object --or write about the people in the picture -- in handsome lettering or hand-drawn text. Enlist family artists to embellish the piece and frame or reproduce it as gifts. Collect memories from the elders of the clan and combine them with photos and drawings, to create a "memory book". Share your family's heritage with others of like background at local ethnic fairs.

Family data can be preserved in many ways. Your emerging sense of drama and story can combine with imagination and other media to take your basic data in completely new directions.

Going Public

You may find, too, that delving into your family's history can provide a jumping-off point into other kinds of history-based writing, and allow you to hone your writing skills with a wider audience. A writer who has researched extensively into a specific place or event because of the family connections to it can try writing a local history. Contact historical societies or museums to learn whether there's interest in this kind of special interest project, and offer to do a brochure or a full-scale book.

If you think your idea might be of interest to an even broader readership, you may want to present it to a commercial publisher. You'll need to have a concrete idea about what you want to say, who might be interested in the topic, and ways in which your project offers a new slant on the subject. Once you've worked this out, you'll need to do still more writing -- a brief query letter in which you propose the project, a longer book proposal describing the direction you plan to take and outlining the complete work, and in most cases, some sample chapters for examination.

But before you rush out to offer your ideas to the world, take a moment to look honestly at your project. Does anyone outside of the family really want to know about your great-great-uncle who built a church in Lynchburg? In other words, does your project have a larger significance that might resonate with people beyond your immediate circle -- or even your local community? If you can look critically at it and still say yes, then check with one of the many writers' guides for models of query letters and book proposals, get a list of likely publishers (see the resource list for all this information) and start writing.

On a smaller scale, though, you can turn your knowledge of history and writing into occasional pieces for local newspapers. Most publications with a strong community orientation welcome material on the region's past, or sketches of significant people or events. Write a short, professional note to the editor, proposing your ideas. Or, if the paper invites unsolicited material from readers, simply write up your piece and send it in.

Other kinds of family material -- anecdotes and memoirs, stories and sayings -- might find a place in one of the small magazines specializing in regional Americana or history. And some historical novelists find that their plots arise from some tidbit of genealogical or historical material. Do you see yourself turning fact into fiction? Your research can pay off in more ways than one.

Offering Your Talents to Others

You aren't the only genealogist who has dreamed of writing the definitive history of a family. The difference, however, may be that you've actually done it. Another way to apply what you've gained from writing your own history is to offer your services to others who aren't able to write their own. Consult, advise, edit -- even offer to write the story for them if you're interested in carrying your efforts that far. And if you've decided to create a small press or publication service to produce your own material, you may want to consider extending the same service to others.

Advertise your services in publications aimed at genealogists; give out flyers and cards at genealogical society meetings. Be prepared for a wide range of projects, and be flexible about your rates. Try to estimate how long it might take you to do the task you're discussing with the client and get any agreement in writing. The best source of information on pricing is the annual *Writer's Market*, which lists a variety of writing tasks and suggested fees.

Practicalities: The Finished Product

Whatever your writing project, there are a number of practical considerations that may arise in the course of getting a text to its readers. You'll find a general discussion of this kind of issue -- legal, ethical and mechanical -- in any comprehensive writing guide. But, since those sources don't focus on the special needs of genealogical writing, we'll take a quick look at some of the most salient concerns for the genealogical storyteller.

Whether you'll be handling all aspects of producing your work, or turning the project over to the professional book producers who -- for a fee -- set the text, print and bind it for you, you'll need a master copy that contains all the material exactly as you want it to appear in the final version. All copies will be made from this master, so it's worth taking the time to ensure that everything is in order and looks precisely as you envisioned it. That's especially important if you're using the local copyshop to produce your text -- no one will do any proofing or altering for you. Larger book production houses, which handle everything from typesetting to binding for the self-publisher, can make changes and reformat text, but it saves steps to have a clean manuscript in precisely the shape you wish.

If you're counting on a small run done via photocopy, make sure that the text is crisp and easy to read, printed on fairly heavy bond paper. If you have the option of selecting a font -- the advent of personal computers puts a range of fonts within reach of nearly every writer, and even many typewriters have interchangeable daisy wheels -- choose a simple, unadorned black letter style. Ornate script-based styles and bold theatrical varieties are fun to experiment with, but they're distracting to the reader and say more about your computer than your writing ability. Aim for a typeface that's similar to that used in books you enjoy reading.

Choosing your typeface wisely can also save you money when it comes to the all-important page count -- important because that's one way to cut costs on the production. Smaller type allows you to fit more text on a page; reducing type size by as little as one point -- keeping it within readable range, of course -- can save several pages' worth of copy costs.

Choose your typeface wisely

If you've produced your text on computer, you can take advantage of the wide range of desktop publishing programs that set up the text in camera-ready form. Even more, pictures and documents can be scanned directly into the appropriate spots in the project -- and then the whole thing is ready to go to the printer.

On the other end of the production scale are those special-interest projects involving hand lettering, artwork and other "special effects." Again, make sure the master looks precisely as you want it to. But more importantly, be sure the printer -- or book producers -- understand how the piece is supposed to look or operate, and that everyone is clear on the potential costs involved for color work and special effects.

Common to all projects, though, are questions of handling the original artifacts that make up those special effects or simply offer a visual counterpart to the text: wills, photos, drawings, maps, letters and any other material that enhances the presentation of your text. Be sure that you don't subject your originals to rough handling or the possibility of loss. Either include disposable copies with your order or book package, or take extra precautions to reduce the risk of losing the original of a family portrait or a crumbling will. Insure them; place them in a special packet, or hand-deliver them to the print shop and wait to pick them up, if it's not possible to make a photocopy. Obviously, don't risk losing or damaging an irreplaceable family heirloom -- even a fat check from the insurance company will do little to console you in the event of a loss.

Legalities: Copyrights and Permissions

What does the law have to do with you at your desk, writing up the stories of your family to send out to all the relatives the world over? Even if you aren't writing for profit, there are legal issues connected with writing that affect you just as much as the famous novelist or syndicated columnist.

The most relevant of these, which touches every writer whose work is meant to be read by others, concerns protection of *copyright* -- your own and that of the materials you use. Copyright law protects writers from unauthorized reproduction of their work, and ensures that they are credited whenever their words appear in someone else's text.

Under current copyright law, all printed materials "in the public domain" can be *reproduced without permission*, though *the sources should always be acknowledged in the text.* For the purposes of genealogical writing, these materials include texts published before the early twentieth century, as well as public records and federal or state government publications. (Take note that materials currently under copyright will have varying expiration dates, due to different laws that have been passed over the years. For specifics, you must contact the office of the Register of Copyrights - see the resource section.) Likewise, the Fair Use Act allows the use of "small amounts" of copyrighted materials for scholarly and non-profit purposes without specific permission from the copyright holder, but it is strongly recommended that you obtain permission anyway. It's easy to write a simple letter requesting permission, and it not only shows your good manners, but it protects you from any possible repercussions and it could help you establish a valuable connection for future projects, thanks to your politeness.

If you're planning to use previously printed material in a commercial project -- to be sold for profit in wider distribution -- or if you're in doubt about whether your project is covered by educational or non-profit use, write first to the the *publisher* of the material in question (usually listed in the front of the book or publication), and request permission to use it. Be specific about author, title, number of pages you want to use, and your purpose in requesting permission. The publisher may own the *publishing rights* to the material you want to use and will also probably be able to contact the *copyright holder* (most likely the author) if necessary. Some publishers may simply give you the name and address of the author and let you pursue it from there. If you've tried contacting the publisher and you're still not sure who the copyright holder is, you may write to the Office of the Register of Copyrights. For a fee ($20.00 at press time), they will perform a copyright check, which basically will tell you the name of the last-known copyright holder, and whether or not the copyright has expired and the work is in the public domain. After all that, you may *still* need to write to the copyright holder and request permission. As you can see, it's best to check with the publisher first, since they can often give you the information you need in one fell swoop, and at no charge to you.

For your own protection, don't take any chances when it comes to copyright infringement. Besides, if you plan to get your work produced by a respectable publisher, they will most certainly demand that you provide the necessary proof of permission before they agree to print a single word.

Remember these two Golden Rules:
- ❑ Honor thy Office of the Register of Copyrights; when in doubt about the copyright status of any printed material you would like to use, request a copyright check.
- ❑ Be sure to ask the permission of others, as you would have them do unto you, when it comes to using previously printed material. This is common courtesy and proper writers' etiquette.

Copyright law also works in your favor. Protecting your own work from unauthorized use is as important for the family historian as it is for the novelist. Whatever form your project takes, you'll want to make sure that it belongs to you, and can't be used without your permission.

The Copyright Act of 1978 makes it simple: your work is copyrighted to you as soon as you write it (because you have created it), and you retain rights to it unless you explicitly sign them away to someone else. All you need to do is to be sure that the word COPYRIGHT, or the copyright symbol, [©] appears on the reverse of the title page, along with the year the material was produced and the name you've chosen to use. To make sure that you have an ironclad defense against plagiarism, you can go a step further and register your copyright -- a matter of requesting the appropriate forms from the Copyright Office of the Library of Congress and filling them out. Once you have returned them, with the obligatory fee ($20.00 in 1994 when this book went to press), your work will be protected against unauthorized reproduction.

The Essentials

The ways to make story from history are as varied as the stories to be told, and people to tell them. While your options may be dictated by factors that are peculiar to your particular circumstances, the best and most enduring texts share a few essential features that character-ize all good genealogical writing:

❏ originality
❏ thematic unity
❏ imagination
❏ reader awareness

Whatever the form your project takes (or may take in the future), you've worked to bridge generations, tie together disparate threads, and invite readers into worlds beyond their experience -- and above all, to celebrate the generations of your family by giving voice to their stories; the stories only you can tell.

HIGHLIGHTS OF PART SIX

- You don't have to stop with just one "family history." There are lots of spin-offs in your material.

- There are avenues for producing your finished work to suit every budget and every plan.

- Family newsletters or special-occasion pieces are inexpensive to produce and distribute.

- Family history writing can lead to published writing in history and fiction.

- It's possible to produce a book inexpensively through your local print shop; make sure you have a camera-ready master copy.

- Whatever form your project takes, be aware of copyright law and restrictions on reproducing published material. Get permission if you've used outside sources.

- All the best genealogy-based writing projects share these features:

  - originality
  - thematic unity
  - imagination
  - reader awareness

PART SEVEN:
Resources

YOUR STORY: A WRITING GUIDE FOR GENEALOGISTS has focused specifically on those writing issues that concern genealogists in their efforts to build a story out of family history material. We've examined basic concepts and strategies for writing strictly in light of their application to the genealogical project, drawing from a wide range of related topics for information on family storytelling. But no single source can ever meet a writer's every need. It takes a combination of resources to cover all aspects of a writing project. Those materials listed below offer expanded coverage of writing and publication questions beyond the scope of this book.

Writing Technique

Guides for writing non-fiction and fiction are readily available in any bookstore and library. They offer suggestions and even exercises for improving writing skills and storytelling technique; some also cover publication. Remember that the issues we've discussed here -- developing theme, structure, and coherence, and so on -- are addressed in books for both non-fiction and writers; you may find more help on description, detail and imagery in those aimed at the short-story writer or novelist. Also included here are standard style manuals for questions on usage and form.

Daigh, Ralph. *Maybe You Should Write a Book.* Englewood Cliffs, N.J.: Prentice-Hall, 1977.

Elbow, Peter. *Writing With Power: Techniques for Mastering the Writing Process.* New York: Oxford University Press, 1981.

Franklin, Jon. *Writing for Story*. New York: Atheneum, 1986.

Knott, Leonard. *Writing for the Joy of It: A Guidebook for Amateurs*. Cincinnati: Writer's Digest Books, 1983.

Mack, Karen and Skjei, Erik. *Overcoming Writing Blocks*. Los Angeles: J. P. Tarcher, 1979.

McGraw-Hill Style Manual. New York: McGraw-Hill, 1983.

Miller, Casey and Swift, Kate. *The Handbook of Non-Sexist Writing*. New York: Barnes & Noble, 1980.

Russ-Larson, Bruce. *Edit Yourself: A Manual for Everyone Who Works With Words*. New York: Norton, 1982.

Shaw, Fran Weber. *30 Ways to Help You Write*. New York: Bantam, 1980.

Tarshis, Barry. *How to Write Like a Pro: A Guide to Effective Nonfiction Writing*. New York: New American Library, 1982.

Venolia, Jan. *Write Right!* Woodland Hills, Calif.: Periwinkle Press, 1979.

Webster's Standard American Style Manual. Springfield, Mass.: Merriam-Webster, Inc., 1985.

Zinsser, William. *On Writing Well*. 4th ed. New York: Harper Collins, 1990.

Family Writing and Research

Interest in family history in its various forms is increasing rapidly; this is reflected in the number of books available on gathering and presenting genealogical material. The resources included here cover a range of topics from research to interviewing. Browse among them for suggestions on new paths to follow, as well as support for the project at hand.

Carlberg, Nancy E. _Becoming a Professional Genealogist._ Anaheim, Calif.: Carlberg Press, 1991.

Daniel, Lois. _How to Write Your Own Life Story: A Step-By-Step Guide for the Non-Professional Writer._ Chicago: Chicago Review Press, 1984.

Dixon, James T. _Preserving Your Past: How to Write Your Autobiography and Family History._ Garden City, N.Y.: Doubleday, 1977.

Dollarhide, William. _Managing a Genealogical Project._ Baltimore: Genealogical Publishing Co., 1991.

Evans, Fanny Maude. _Changing Memories Into Memoirs: A Guide to Writing Your Life Story._ New York: Barnes & Noble, 1984.

Fletcher, William. _Recording Your Family History._ Berkeley, Calif.: Ten Speed Press, 1989.

Lackey, Richard S. _Cite Your Sources._ Jackson, Miss.: University Press of Mississippi, 1986.

Lomask, Milton. _The Biographer's Craft._ New York: Harper & Row, 1986.

Neagles, James. _The Library of Congress: A Guide to Genealogical & Historical Research._ Salt Lake City: Ancestry, 1990.

Rivers, William L. _Finding Facts: Interviewing, Observing, Using Reference Sources._ Englewood Cliffs, N. J.: Prentice-Hall, 1975.

Rosenbluth, Vera. *Keeping Family Stories Alive: A Creative Guide to Taping Your Family Life and Love.* Point Roberts, Wash.: Hartley & Marks, Inc., 1990.

Sheehy, Eugene P., compiler. *Guide to Reference Books.* Chicago: American Library Association, annually.

Todd, Alden. *Finding Facts Fast: How to Find Out What You Want and Need to Know.* Berkeley, Calif.: Ten Speed Press, 1979.

Zimmerman, William. *Instant Oral Biographies: How to Interview People and Tape the Stories of Their Lives.* New York: Guaironex Press, 1981.

Manuscript Preparation and Publishing

Now that desktop publishing and copyshops have put book production and distribution within the reach of nearly every writer, many sources are available for guidance on managing all aspects of producing your work. Among the resources below you'll find detailed information on preparing, printing and distributing your work, as well as specifics on copyright and legalities.

Applebaum, Judith and Nancy Evans. _How to Get Happily Published._ New York: Harper & Row, 1978.

Armstrong, Donald. _Donald Armstrong's Complete Book Publishing Handbook._ Houston: D. Armstrong Co., 1989.

Barker, Malcolm. _Book Design & Production for the Small Publisher: A Do-It-Yourself Guide._ San Francisco: Londonborn Publications, 1990.

Brownstone, David M. and Irene M. Franck. _The Self-Publishing Handbook._ New York: New American Library, 1981.

Burke, Clifford. _Printing It: A Guide to Graphic Techniques for the Impecunious._ Berkeley, Calif.: Wingbow Press, 1972.

Doty, Betty. _Publish Your Own Handbound Books._ Redding, Calif.: The Bookery, 1980.

Hasselstrom, L. M. _The Book Book: A Publishing Handbook for Beginners and Others._ Hermosa, S.Dak.: Lame Johnny Press, 1979.

Hudson, Howard Penn. _Publishing Newsletters._ New York: Scribner's, 1988.

Lind, Marilyn. _Printing and Publishing Your Family History._ Cloquet, Minn.: Linden Tree, 1986.

McGrady, L. J. _How to Publish Your Genealogy._ Toledo, Ohio: L. J. McGrady, 1984.

Pocket Pal: A Graphic Arts Production Handbook. 12th ed. New York: International Paper Co., 1979.

Poynter, Dan. *Publishing Short-Run Books: How to Paste Up and Reproduce Books Instantly Using Your Quick Print Shop.* Santa Barbara, Calif.: Para Publishing, 1988.

Register of Copyrights, Library of Congress, Washington, D.C., 20559.

Stone, Bernard and Arthur Eckstein. *Preparing Art for Printing.* New York: Van Nostrand Reinhold, 1983.

White, Jan V. *Mastering Graphics: Design and Production Made Easy.* New York: Bowker, 1983.

Epilogue

*T*he books listed here represent only a fraction of the resources which can be used in conjunction with *YOUR STORY* to provide a multifaceted picture of genealogical storytelling. These are, however, most compatible with the approach to writing taken in this book. Use these and other how-to books and writing guides at need to answer questions that arise in the course of your writing, but don't confine your research to texts like these. The best way to understand how stories work is to read them.

Historical texts, folktales, novels, short stories, poems, vignettes... All these expose you to story models and get your creativity flowing. Your family history is no less valid a subject for story than an author's invented characters and setting. Read aloud to make your language sing. Follow your imagination wherever it goes: every idea, every image, every kind of writing is fair game for investigation and even emulation, as long as it helps you free the stories within your family's past.

Index

About the Author

Carla Jean Eardley is a writer, artist and longtime teacher of English and writing, whose prose and poetry have appeared in a number of national journals and magazines. She writes and consults on genealogical and historical projects for private clients -- experiences which laid the foundations for this book. Carla Jean Eardley lives in Tucson, Arizona, where she also teaches writing and family storytelling classes, and operates her own lettering and design studio.

www.ingramcontent.com/pod-product-compliance
Lightning Source LLC
Chambersburg PA
CBHW071230290326
41931CB00037B/2570